--

101 SCRIPTURAL PROOFS
for the
PRE-TRIBULATION
RAPTURE

C.M. BOYER

Also by the author:

The NEPHILIM DECEPTION

101 SCRIPTURAL PROOFS
for the
PRE-TRIBULATION
RAPTURE

C.M. BOYER
BS, Business Management and Economics,
SUNY—Saratoga Springs.
Former technical writer and editor for Fortune 100
companies operating internationally.
Former U.S. Government operational
intelligence analyst.

Published by Create Space
an Amazon company

101 SCRIPTURAL PROOFS
for the
PRE-TRIBULATION
RAPTURE

Second Edition 2017

© **2016, 2017 C.M. Boyer**. All Rights Reserved. Except as permitted by the Copyright Act of 1976, no part of this publication may be reproduced, stored in a retrieval system or transmitted in any form or by any means without the prior written permission of the publisher.

Cover art background
by charlotte_202003
@ pixabay.com

Boyer, C.M.
101 Scriptural Proofs for the Pre-Tribulation Rapture 2nd Edition / by C.M. Boyer
1.United States. 2. Non-fiction.
ISBN-13: 978-1981889372
ISBN-10: 198188937X

"The Bible is worth all the other books which have ever been printed."
--Patrick Henry

INTRODUCTION

Many people have heard of "The Rapture." Some think it is folly or fiction. Others in Christendom believe it is a "new doctrine." However, it is one of the oldest teachings in Scripture.

One thing many in the Christian faith agree on is that the Rapture will happen, but there is confusion about its timing. Some believe in a Pre-Tribulation Rapture; others in a Mid-Tribulation Rapture. Strangely, some people believe in an End of Tribulation Rapture. (Even stranger, there are those who believe we are living in Christ's Millennial Reign Kingdom.)

There is also confusion between the Rapture and Jesus' return to earth in the 2nd Advent. When people say "Jesus is returning soon" they are speaking of His 2nd Advent. But they neglect to account for the fact that the 70th Week of Daniel—known as the Tribulation Period--must run its course beforehand.

This book sets forth overwhelming Scriptural evidence that proves a Pre-Tribulation Rapture of Christ's followers. Exhaustive research was conducted to ensure a "Scripture compared with Scripture" approach to the subject. Old and New Testament references to a Pre-Tribulation Rapture are compared and presented in context. Links are provided to commentary from respected pastors and Bible scholars.

The reason for the 7-year Tribulation Period is also discussed in depth presenting evidence from the Old Testament book of Daniel Chapter 9 known as "The Key to All End Times Prophecy." In light of this prophecy the modern sign posts that start God's "Prophetic time Clock" and signal the imminence of the Pre-Tribulation Rapture are presented.

Abundant evidence for the Pre-Tribulation Rapture contained in the book of Revelation is discussed in depth as well.

THE "APOCALYPSE" MEANS "UNVEILING" or REVEALING

Apocalypse is derived from the Greek word apokalypsis. Although it's often used to describe a great devastation or cataclysm, the literal meaning of apocalypse is actually an unveiling, or revealing. [Bible Study - What Does Apocalypse Really Mean? www.keyway.ca/htm2003/20031008.htm Oct 8, 2003 -]

As can be clearly seen from Chapter 1 of the book of Revelation, it's all about Jesus, His Story (history), which He gives us ahead of time in Prophecy, as seen from Revelation Chapter 1:

{1:1} The Revelation of Jesus Christ, which God gave unto him, to shew unto his servants things which must shortly come to pass; and he sent and signified [it] by his angel unto his servant John: {1:2} Who bare record of the word of God, and of

the testimony of Jesus Christ, and of all things that he saw. {1:3} Blessed [is] he that readeth, and they that hear the words of this prophecy, and keep those things which are written therein: for the time [is] at hand.{1:4} John to the seven churches which are in Asia: Grace[be] unto you, and peace, from him which is, and which was, and which is to come; and from the seven Spirits which are before his throne; {1:5} And from Jesus Christ,[who is] the faithful witness, [and] the first begotten of the dead, and the prince of the kings of the earth. Unto him that loved us, and washed us from our sins in his own blood,{1:6} And hath made us kings and priests unto God and his Father; to him [be] glory and dominion for ever and ever. Amen. {1:7} Behold, he cometh with clouds; and every eye shall see him, and they [also] which pierced him: and all kindreds of the earth shall wail because of him. Even so, Amen.

{1:8} I am Alpha and Omega, the beginning and the ending, saith the Lord, which is, and which was, and which is to come, the Almighty.

CONTENTS

CHAPTER 1: DISTINCTION BETWEEN THE RAPTURE AND CHRIST'S 2ND ADVENT........1

Rapture Defined	1
The Twinkling of an Eye	3
Not a New Doctrine	4
Distinction Between the Rapture and Christ's 2nd Advent	5
Rapture: Christ's Coming/Appearing Only for His Followers	5
The "Secret Rapture"	10
The Trumpet Voice: the Call to "Come up Hither"	11
This Trumpet Call is the "Last Trump" of 1 Corinthians 15	12
Believers Saved from Wrath	14
No Mid-Tribulation Rapture	15
No Rapture (or Trumpet Call) After the Tribulation	16
Those Who Died in Christ Before the Rapture Christ Will Bring with Him	17
What Kind of Body After Rapture?	18
Rapture Happens on "The Day of Christ"	19
The Day of Christ Same as The Lord's Day?	19
No Rapture for General Population	22
2nd Advent: Jesus Returns to Earth with all His Raptured Followers	23
WORKS CITED & SCRIPTURE REFERENCED	24

CHAPTER 2: REASON FOR THE TRIBULATION IS OPPOSITE THE REASON FOR THE RAPTURE 26

Tribulation Defined	27
Church Age Ends, Trials and Judgment Begin	28
The OT Book of Daniel Provides the Basis for the Tribulation	29
Daniel 9:24: "The Key to All End Times Prophecy"	31
70 Weeks Determined	31

1. The Going Forth of the Commandment to Restore and Build Jerusalem 32
2. Unto Messiah the Prince: Jesus 33
3. Messiah "Cut Off": Jesus Rejected 34
God's "Prophetic Time Clock" Stopped 35
Jews Dispersed and Later Re-Gathered to Israel 36
7 Years Remain to be Fulfilled 37
The Tribulation is to "Finish the Transgression..." 37
Reason for the Rapture is Opposite the Reason for the Tribulation 38
Believers Not Appointed to Wrath 38
The Church is the Lord's Bride--And His Body 40
WORKS CITED & SCRIPTURE REFERENCED 42

CHAPTER 3: ISRAEL AND DANIEL'S 70TH WEEK..44

Salvation From the Jews and To the Jew First 44
70th Week Distinctly Jewish in Nature 47
Approximate 2,000 Year Interval Between Diaspora and 1948 48
The Coming One Week Covenant: the Remaining 7 Years 49
Psalm 83 War and the Commandment to "Restore and Build Jerusalem" 50
Start of the 70th Week: Covenant with Anti-Christ 52
First 3 1/2 Years of Tribulation Fairly Peaceful 53
Mid-Week: Anti-Christ Breaks the Covenant 54
Last 3 1/2 Years: "Time of Jacob's Troubles" 55
End of the Tribulation: Christ's 2nd Advent 55
3 Signs of the Imminent Rapture 56
Parable of the Fig Tree 57
SCRIPTURE REFERENCED 58

CHAPTER 4: RAPTURE PRE-FIGURED IN THE OLD AND NEW TESTAMENTS..........................60

Old Testament Raptures and Pre-Figures
of the Pre-Tribulation Rapture 61
Enoch Raptured 61
Noah & Family Delivered 62
Lot & His 2 Daughters Delivered 62
Rahab & Family Delivered 63
Elijah Raptured 63
Isaiah: Pre-Tribulation Rapture for Saint's
Protection 64
Zechariah: After Tribulation Raptured Return to Earth 64
New Testament Records Several Individuals Raptured 65
Jesus Raptured at Ascension 65
Paul and John Raptured 65
Lord's Two Witnesses Raptured at End of Their Witness 66
Gospels Speak of Calling Up/Away of Christ's Followers 67
Matthew 24:37 67
Matthew 25: Parable of 10 Virgins 69
Luke 21:36 72
Why John's Gospel Omits Olivet Discourse 72
Epistles Speak of Pre-Tribulation Rapture 73
Paul's Epistles 73
Peter's Epistle 75
John's Epistle 75
Jude's Epistle 76
Raptures & Saving From Judgment Indicate
Begin/End of Dispensations 76
Book of Revelation: Much Evidence for
Pre-Tribulation Rapture 80
WORKS CITED & SCRIPTURE REFERENCED 81

CHAPTER 5: REVELATION PROVIDES MOST EVIDENCE FOR A PRE-TRIB RAPTURE........83

Specific Statements Point to Pre-Tribulation Rapture 85
"The Lord's Day" in Chapter 1 85
Jesus Promises to Keep Followers from Tribulation 86

Parenthetical Structure of 6-18: Church Not Mentioned Throughout	87
Divisions of the Book	89
Chapter 19 "And after these things"	91
Chapters 1, 2 & 3: Change of Speakers / Locale	93
Chapter 12: All About Israel	94
Chapter 16--Problematic?	97
Reason for Tribulation: Big Proof of Pre-Tribulation Rapture	99
The 144,000 Witnesses of Revelation 7 are Jewish	100
The 144,000 are Martyred for Their Testimony of Jesus	101
Chapter 19: The Church is Christ's Heavenly Bride Who Returns to Earth with Him	102
WORKS CITED & SCRIPTURE REFERENCED	103

CHAPTER 6: SYMBOLISM IN THE BOOK OF REVELATION..105

John Symbolic of all Believers	106
7 Spirits are Complete Work of Holy Spirit in the Church	107
7 Churches Symbolize Complete Church Age	107
24 Elders Symbolize All the Redeemed	109
Old Testament Pre-Figure of 24 Elders	110
The Beast of Revelation Chapter 13 is Entire Un-Redeemed World	113
Conglomerate of Daniel's Beasts	115
Satan is Behind the Beast	117
The Beast is Scarlet--Symbolic of Sin	121
Anti-Christ is "Little Horn" per Daniel	123
God's Beasts Around Throne Counter to World's Beast	127
Martyrs of Revelation 7:9 Clothed in White	130
John a Pre-Trib Believer Doesn't Recognize Martyrs	130
God's Wrath Finally Poured Out	133
"It is Done": No Post-Tribulation Rapture	135
Mystery Babylon: Confusion	137
Believers Think Opposite of Mystery Babylon	139
Symbolic Harlot: False Religion of Sacrifice	140
Mystery Babylon The Great: Worldly Commercial System	142

That Great City: Jerusalem	142
Symbolic Sodom and Egypt	143
The Hour that Will Try the Whole World	144
WORKS CITED & SCRIPTURE REFERENCED	147

CHAPTER 7: JESUS THE THIEF RAPTURES HIS FOLLOWERS 149

Jesus--The Thief in the Night	149
Day of the Lord: Rapture and the Start of the Tribulation	149
"Night" Symbolic of Spiritual Darkness	150
Night Comes Upon People Unaware	151
Believers Walk in the Day	152
WORKS CITED & SCRIPTURE REFERENCED	154

CONCLUSION... 155

101 (PLUS) PROOFS ENUMERATED............ 156

SOURCES & REFERENCES......................... 163

READER'S NOTES...................................... 165

CHAPTER 1: DISTINCTION BETWEEN THE RAPTURE AND CHRIST'S 2ND ADVENT

- Rapture Defined
- The Twinkling of an Eye
- Not a New Doctrine
- Distinction Between the Rapture and Christ's 2nd Advent
- Rapture: Christ's Coming/Appearing Only for His Followers
- The "Secret Rapture"
- The Trumpet Voice: the Call to "Come up Hither"
- This Trumpet Call is the "Last Trump" of 1 Corinthians 15
- Believers Saved from Wrath
- No Mid-Tribulation Rapture
- No Rapture (or Trumpet Call) After the Tribulation
- Those Who Died in Christ Before the Rapture Christ Will Bring with Him
- What Kind of Body After Rapture?
- Rapture Happens on "The Day of Christ"
- The Day of Christ Same as The Lord's Day
- No Rapture for General Population
- 2nd Advent: Jesus Returns to Earth with all His Raptured Followers

Rapture Defined

The word Rapture does not appear in English translations of Scripture. In the original Greek manuscripts the word "harpazo" was used as a verb. According to Strong's Concordance harpazo means: "to seize, catch up, snatch away, obtain by robbery" [1]. This word harpazo was translated from the Greek to "raptume" (or "raeptius" or "raptureo" depending on the usage) in the Latin Bible and this is where we get the word Rapture. The Greek lexicon based on Thayer's and Smith's Bible Dictionary [2] gives examples of where in the Bible the word harpazo or a form of it is used. The following is by the apostle Paul in 2 Corinthians:

12:2 "I knew a man in Christ above fourteen years ago, ... such an one caught up to the third heaven."

In Latin "caught up" is translated *raptume*; in Greek it is translated *harpagenta*.

The Merriam Webster Dictionary defines Rapture as:

"1: an expression or manifestation of ecstasy or passion; 2 a: a state or experience of being carried away by overwhelming emotion b: a mystical experience in which the spirit is exalted to a knowledge of divine things; 3 often capitalized: the final assumption of Christians into heaven during the end-time according to Christian theology" [3].

No doubt all three of the above definitions would be fit to describe the feeling of being caught up or called up to Heaven by the Lord Jesus.

The Twinkling of an Eye

Paul writes in 1 Corinthians 15:51-54 that the Rapture will happen in the twinkling of an eye:

"Behold, I shew you a mystery; We shall not all sleep, but we shall all be changed, In a moment, in the twinkling of an eye, at the last trump: for the trumpet shall sound, and the dead shall be raised incorruptible, and we shall be changed."

This will be fast, as "the twinkling of an eye" refers to the speed that light reflects off of the eye:

Meters per second: 299792458

Miles per second: 186000

Miles per hour: 671 million (6.71×10^8).

Not a New Doctrine

Scripture mentions several cases where people were raptured or taken up to Heaven by God because they were His devoted followers. A "rapture" is in fact one of the oldest teachings in Scripture. Both the Old Testament (OT) and New Testament (NT) speak of God's people being raptured.

Enoch in Genesis 5:24 was the first person raptured. Elijah in 2 Kings Chapter 2 was also raptured. Other Old Testament saints have been saved out of judgment and are pre-figures of a Pre-Tribulation Rapture.

In the NT several people have been raptured: Jesus at His Ascension; Paul, as he mentioned in 2 Corinthians; the apostle John in Revelation Chapter 1, and the Lord's two Witnesses of Revelation Chapter 11.

These examples of individuals having been raptured are discussed further in CHAPTER 4. From the aforementioned, it is clear that the Rapture is not a new doctrine.

Distinction Between the Rapture and Christ's 2nd Advent

When people say "Jesus will return soon" they neglect to account for the fact that there will be at least 7 years between the time they've said that and the Lord's return. That is because the Rapture of Christ's followers must take place first, and then at some point thereafter the 7-year Tribulation Period must undergo its determined course before the Lord's 2nd Advent.

It's important to maintain this distinction between Christ's coming/appearing for His followers in the Rapture and His 2nd Advent to earth to rule and reign after the Tribulation. The reason for the Tribulation sheds light on this and is discussed more fully in CHAPTER 2.

Rapture: Christ's Coming/Appearing Only for His Followers

The Scriptures that speak of the "appearing/coming" of the Lord for His saints at the Rapture speak only to His followers—not the general population. In contrast the Scriptures that speak of the Lord's 2nd Advent show that His followers return to earth with Him and those "left behind" do not welcome His return. [Luke 23:30, Revelation 6:16].

The apostle Paul uses the words "coming" and "appearing" to refer to the Lord Jesus at the Rapture. In the following statements Paul uses the word "coming" to describe Jesus at the Rapture:

1 Thessalonians 2:19: "For what is our hope, or joy, or crown of rejoicing? Are not even ye in the presence of our Lord Jesus Christ at his coming?"

Here Paul will rejoice seeing fellow believers with him as they are taken up to Christ's Kingdom. Paul cannot be speaking about the end of the Tribulation Period since Paul has been bodily dead for centuries, but right after he died he was immediately spiritually present with Jesus, as he explains in 2 Corinthians 5:8:

"To be absent from the body is to be present with the lord."

Like Paul, when anyone who is a follower of Jesus dies they are not kept in an unconscious state; rather, their souls are immediately with the Lord.

In 1 Thess. 5:5 Paul says:

"And the very God of peace sanctify you wholly; and I pray God your whole spirit and soul and body be preserved blameless unto the coming of our Lord Jesus Christ."

Paul expounds upon this in 1 Thess. 4:17:

"Then we which are alive and remain shall be caught up together with them in the clouds, to meet the Lord in the air: and so shall be ever be with the Lord"

Again, the aforementioned can't be at the end of the Tribulation because at that time God does not call anyone up to Him; instead, all of Jesus' saints follow Him *from* Heaven *to* earth as Revelation 19:14 attests:

"And the armies which were in heaven followed him upon white horses, clothes in fine linen, white and clean."

If, then, the Lord's followers return to earth with Him, it should follow that they were residents with Him in the Kingdom of Heaven during the Tribulation.

In the following statements Paul uses the word "appearing" to refer to the Lord Jesus at the Rapture:

1 Timothy 6:14: "That thou keep [this] commandment without spot, unrebukeable, until the appearing of our Lord Jesus Christ..."

2 Tim. 1:10: "But is now made manifest by the appearing of our Saviour Jesus Christ who hath abolished death, and hath brought life and immortality to light through the gospel..."

2 Tim. 4:1: "I charge [thee] therefore before God, and the Lord Jesus Christ, who shall judge the quick and the dead at his appearing and his kingdom..." (This statement indicates the Lord will judge His followers at His appearing and the dead at the Great White Throne Judgment [Rev. 20:11] in His Kingdom.)

Titus 2:13: "*Looking for that blessed hope, and the glorious appearing the great God and our Savior Jesus Christ.*"

Peter and John use the words "appear," "appearing" and "revelation" to describe the Lord Jesus at the Rapture:

1 Peter 1:7: "*That the trial of your faith, being much more precious than of gold that perished, thought it be tried with fire, might be found unto praise and honour and glory at the appearing of Jesus Christ.*"

1 Pet. 1:13: "*Wherefore gird up the loins of your mind, be sober, and hope to the end for the grace that is to be brought unto you at the revelation of Jesus Christ.*"

1 Pet. 5:21: "*And when the chief Shepard shall appear, ye shall receive a crown of glory that fadeth not away.*"

This crown is mentioned by Paul in 2 Timothy 4:8 and shown worn by believers in Heaven with the Lord during the Tribulation [Rev.4:4].

1 John 3:2: "Beloved, now we are the sons of God, and it doth not yet appear what we shall be: but we know that, when he shall appear, we shall be like him: for we shall see him as he is."

The "Secret Rapture"

As mentioned previously, only the followers of the Lord Jesus will be raptured, as Paul in 2 Timothy 4:8 attests:

"Henceforth there is laid up for me a crown of righteousness, which the Lord, the righteous judge, shall give me at that day: and not to me only, but unto all them also that love his appearing."

This appearing of Jesus only for those "that love his appearing" is what some have termed the "Secret Rapture." In one aspect it is, because while those "left behind" will witness it, the rapture is only for those who are awaiting Christ, have "ears to hear" [Luke 8:8], are attuned to the Lord's voice, as John 10:27 attests:

"My sheep hear my voice, and I know them, and they follow me..."

The Trumpet Voice: the Call to "Come Up Hither"

The Lord uses this Voice to call up John to Heaven in Revelation 4:1-3:

*"After this I looked, and, behold, a door was opened in heaven: and the first voice which I heard was as it were of a trumpet talking with me; which said, **Come up hither**, and I will shew thee things which must be hereafter."*

"And immediately I was in the spirit: and, behold, a throne was set in heaven, and one sat on the throne. And he that sat was to look upon like a jasper and a sardine stone: and there was a rainbow round about the throne, in sight like unto an emerald."

The call to "Come up hither" is the trumpet Voice the Lord's followers will hear when they are raptured. This "Rapture call" is indeed the issued to the Lord's two Witnesses of Revelation Chapter 11. After they are slain, the world throws a big party, rejoicing over their dead bodies lying in the streets. But after 3 ½ days the Lord says "Come up hither" and they are taken back up into Heaven.

This Trumpet Call is the "Last Trump" of 1 Corinthians 15

The Rapture Call to *Come up hither* is the "last trump" of 1 Corinthians 15:51-54. If God can make His voice sound like it is "walking" in Genesis 3:8:

"And they heard the voice of the LORD God walking in the garden in the cool of the day..."

...He can make it sound like a trumpet, as in Revelation 1:20-22:

"I was in the Spirit on the Lord's day, and heard behind me a great voice, as of a trumpet, Saying, I am Alpha and Omega, the first and the last:..."

...as in Exodus 19:16:

"And it came to pass on the third day in the morning, that there were thunders and lightnings, and a thick cloud upon the mount, and the voice of the trumpet exceeding loud; so that all the people that was in the camp trembled."

Some argue that the "last trump" refers to the final trumpet judgment during the Tribulation. In Revelation 8:13; however, we read that the trumpet judgments bring "woe" (never ending misery) to the inhabiters of the earth:

"And I beheld, and heard an angel flying through the midst of heaven, saying with a loud voice, Woe, woe, woe, to the inhabiters of the earth by reason of the other voices of the trumpet of the three angels, which are yet to sound!"

Revelation Chapter 8 is parenthetical with Chapter 15, meaning that it is 7 chapters apart in the narrative but these chapters—8 and 15--should be read consecutively. This parenthetical structure of the Revelation narrative is explained more fully in CHAPTER 5 under the heading "Parenthetical Structure of 6-18: Church Not Mentioned Throughout."

The last trumpet judgment is sounded in Rev. 11:15. Since Chapter 11 of Revelation is parenthetical to Chapter 18, this is at the very end of the Tribulation:

"And the seventh angel sounded; and there were great voices in heaven, saying, The kingdoms of this world are become the kingdoms of our Lord, and of his Christ; and he shall reign for ever and ever."

This last trumpet sounding--like the others before it--brings "woe" to all the people on earth. If Christians were on earth at this time they too would suffer this "never ending misery." Instead, as the previous Scripture attests, the saints are in Heaven saying *"The kingdoms of this world are become the kingdoms of our Lord..."*

Believers Saved from Wrath

The Tribulation is a time of mankind's wrath toward one another (Rev. 18, since in v. 13 we see that people have engaged in the selling of slaves and the souls of men); a time of Satan's wrath against the Jews (and the world in general) [Rev. 12:12], and finally after much patience, a time of God's wrath toward the unrepentant [Rev.

16:17]. But believers are not appointed to wrath as Paul states in Romans 5:9-11:

"Much more then, being now justified by his blood, we shall be saved from wrath through him. For if, when we were enemies, we were reconciled to God by the death of his Son, much more, being reconciled, we shall be saved by his life. And not only [so], but we also joy in God through our Lord Jesus Christ, by whom we have now received the atonement."

No Mid-Tribulation Rapture

Revelation Chapters 6-18 which cover events in the Tribulation period provide no evidence for a mid-Tribulation Rapture. In fact, "Mid-Week" (halfway through the 7 year period known as the 70th Week of Daniel) the anti-Christ begins to severely persecute the Jews. He kills the ones sealed with God's Holy Spirit, as well as all those who accept their witness of Jesus as Savior [Rev. 7:9].

No Rapture (or Trumpet Call) After the Tribulation

In Matthew 24:29-31 the Lord talks about the things that will occur immediately after the Tribulation: 1) the Son of man will appear in heaven; 2) all the people on earth will <u>mourn</u> because of this; 3) He will come to the earth with power and great glory; 4) His angels will gather his elect from one end of heaven to the other. Jesus says nothing about "calling up" his followers from the earth to Heaven since they're all over heaven at this time:

"Immediately after the tribulation of those days shall the sun be darkened, and the moon shall not give her light, and the stars shall fall from heaven, and the powers of the heavens shall be shaken: And then shall appear the sign of the Son of man in heaven: and then shall all the tribes of the earth mourn, and they shall see the Son of man coming in the clouds of heaven with power and great glory. And he shall send his angels with a great sound of a trumpet, and they shall gather together his elect from the four winds, from one end of heaven to the other."

It is important to note that the above Scripture says that the elect (followers of Jesus) aren't gathered from the earth, but from *"One end of heaven to the other."*

The only people who are raptured near the end of the Tribulation period are the two Witnesses in Revelation Chapter 11—who were sent to earth from Heaven. These two are issued the same call to "Come up hither" as the Lord's followers at the Rapture, as shown by John being called to "Come up hither" in Revelation Chapter 1. In CHAPTER 5 I show that John is symbolic of all pre-Tribulation, Church Age believers.

Those Who Died in Christ Before the Rapture Christ Will Bring with Him

Paul in 1 Thessalonians 4:13-16 says:

"But I would not have you to be ignorant, brethren, concerning them which are asleep, that ye sorrow not, even as others which have no hope. For if we believe that Jesus died and rose again,

even so them also which sleep in Jesus wills God bring with him. For this we say unto you by the word of the Lord, that we which are alive and remain unto the coming the Lord shall not prevent them which are asleep."

What Kind of Body After Rapture? In Philippians 3:21 Paul explains what kind of body the followers of Jesus will receive once present with Him, stating that the Lord

"...shall change our vile body that it may be fashioned like unto his glorious body, according to the working whereby he is able even to subdue all things unto himself."

This body will be like the Lord's as John describes Jesus in the Book of Revelation [1:12-16], and which was shown to John, Andrew, Peter and James in the Transfiguration [Matthew 17:2, Mark 9:2-3]. Jesus' followers who have died prior to the Rapture will be resurrected into new, glorious bodies at the Rapture.

Rapture Happens on "The Day of Christ"

The Rapture occurs on "the day of Christ" which the apostle Paul speaks of:

Philippians 1:10 "That ye may approve things that are excellent; that ye may be sincere and without offence till the day of Christ;"

Phil. 2:16 "Holding forth the word of life; that I may rejoice in the day of Christ, that I have not run in vain, neither laboured in vain:"

2 Thess. 2:2 "That ye be not soon shaken in mind, or be troubled, neither by spirit, nor by word, nor by letter as from us, as that the day of Christ is at hand."

The Day of Christ Same as The Lord's Day?

The Day of Christ maybe be the same as "the Lord's Day" --a Sunday (1st day of the week)-- which was His day of Resurrection. John states of the Lord's Day in Revelation 1:10:

"I was in the Spirit on the Lord's day, and heard behind me a great voice, as of a trumpet, ..."

Pastor Cornelius R. Stam in his article "The Day of the Lord, What is it?" [4] argues that the Rapture precedes the Lord's Day which includes the Tribulation period:

"...I Thessalonians 5:1-3 states that the 'destruction of 'the day of the Lord' will also come as 'a thief in the night.' The Antichrist will have made a seven-year covenant with Israel and the world will enjoy three and a half years of 'peace and safety.' Then, unexpectedly, he will break the covenant and defile the temple, plunging the nations into the most terrible time of trouble they have ever experienced..."

Will anyone be saying, 'Peace and safety' at the close of the 'great tribulation'... as the battle of Armageddon rages? How, then, can this passage about 'the day of the Lord' refer only to the return of Christ after the tribulation? But when we see that 'the day of the Lord' begins with, rather than after the tribulation, all is in order."

A link to Pastor Stam's article is provided in the appendix to this Chapter.

The OT book of Zechariah speaks of the Lord's Day in Chapter 14:1-5:

"Behold, the day of the Lord cometh...For I will gather all nations against Jerusalem to battle...Then shall the Lord go forth and fight against those nations (Rev. 19:17)...And his feet shall stand in that day upon the mount of Olives...and the mount...shall cleave in the midst (referring to the great earthquake in Revelation 16:18)...and the Lord my God shall come, and all the saints with thee(at the end of the Tribulation)."

In Revelation Chapter 3:11 the Lord states *"Behold, I come quickly...."* He repeats this in Revelation 22:7 and 22:12. This "quickly" is in context of the entirety of the Lord's Day, since it has been 1,900-plus years since John wrote what the Lord advised him to in AD 90. The Lord interjects this phrase after He promises to keep those in the Philadelphia-type church from the Tribulation. In 22:12 the Lord adds *"...and my reward is with me..."* meaning His followers. These are two proofs of the Pre-Tribulation Rapture.

No Rapture for the General Population

As mentioned, only the Lord's followers will be raptured. Scripture provides evidence against a rapture for those who don't follow Christ. In His address to the 7 Churches in Revelation Chapters 3 and 4 the Lord cautions several "church types" to repent. In particular He tells the church of Thyatira in Revelation 2:22:

"Behold, I will cast her into a bed, and them that commit adultery with her into great tribulation, except they repent of their deeds."

As mentioned, those who have been "left behind" will not welcome Jesus' return. Scripture tells us that at the end of the Tribulation people on earth are not happy about the Lord's return and they hide under rocks and in caves yelling *"...hide us...from the wrath of the Lamb"* [Rev. 6:16]. Other deluded souls try to fight against Him, and they are slain by the sword of His Word [Rev. 19:19-21].

2nd Advent: Jesus Returns to Earth with all His Raptured Followers

As seen from Revelation 19:14 Jesus comes to earth with a great multitude of Heavenly residents following Him:

"And the armies which were in heaven followed him upon white horses, clothed in fine linen, white and clean."

Zechariah in the Old Testament prophesied of this long ago in Chapter 14:4-5:

"And his feet shall stand in that day upon the Mount of Olives...and there shall be a very great valley; and half of the mountain shall remove toward the north, and half of it toward the south. And ye shall flee to the valley of the mountains....and the Lord my God shall come, and all the saints with thee."

This makes clear that Christ's 2nd Advent to earth is *after* the Tribulation period and that there is no Post-Tribulation Rapture.

WORKS CITED & SCRIPTURE REFERENCED IN CHAPTER 1

[1] Strong's Concordance harpazó: to seize, catch up, snatch… obtain by robbery…snatch up, suddenly and decisively – like someone seizing bounty (spoil, a prize); to take by an open display of force (i.e. not covertly or secretly). http://biblehub.com/greek/726.htm

[2] **HARPAZO the KJV New Testament Greek Lexicon.** Greek lexicon based on Thayer's and Smith's Bible Dictionary plus others; this is keyed to the large Kittel and the "Theological Dictionary of the New Testament." http://www.biblestudytools.com/lexicons/greek/kjv/harpazo.html

[3] **Merriam-Webster Dictionary.** http://www.merriam-webster.com/dictionary/rapture

[4] **Pastor Cornelius R. Stam.** The Day of the Lord — What Is It? On September 2, 2001 @ 8:57 pm **https://www.bereanbiblesociety.org/the-day-of-the-lord-what-is-it/**

Luke 23:30 Then shall they begin to say to the mountains, Fall on us; and to the hills, Cover us.

Rev. 6:16 And said to the mountains and rocks, Fall on us, and hide us from the face of him that sitteth on the throne, and from the wrath of the Lamb:

Rev. 20:11 And I saw a great white throne, and him that sat on it, from whose face the earth and the heaven fled away; and there was found no place for them.

Rev. 4:4 And round about the throne were four and twenty seats: and upon the seats I saw four and twenty elders sitting, clothed in white raiment; and they had on their heads crowns of gold.

Luke 8:8 ...And when he had said these things, he cried, He that hath ears to hear, let him hear.

Rev. 12:12 Therefore rejoice, ye heavens, and ye that dwell in them. Woe to the inhabiters of the earth and of the sea! for the devil is come down unto you, having great wrath, because he knoweth that he hath but a short time.

Rev. 16:17 And the seventh angel poured out his vial into the air; and there came a great voice out of the temple of heaven, from the throne, saying, It is done.

Rev. 7:9 After this I beheld...a great multitude...of all nations, and kindreds, and people, and tongues, stood before the throne, and before the Lamb, clothed with white robes, and palms in their hands;

Rev. 1:12-16 And I turned to see....one like unto the Son of man, ...His head and his hairs were white like wool... and his eyes were as a flame of fire; ...his feet like unto fine brass,... and his voice as the sound of many waters... and his countenance was as the sun shineth in his strength.

Matt. 17:2 And was transfigured before them: and his face did shine as the sun, and his raiment was white as the light.

Mark 9:2-3 ...Jesus taketh with him Peter, and James, and John, and...he was transfigured before them. And his raiment became shining, exceeding white as snow; so as no fuller on earth can white them.

Mark 9:2-3 ...and he was transfigured before them. And his raiment became shining, exceeding white...

Rev. 19:19-21 And I saw the beast...and with him the false prophet ...both were cast alive into a lake of fire burning with brimstone. And the remnant were slain with the sword of him that sat upon the horse, which sword proceeded out of his mouth: and all the fowls were filled with their flesh.

CHAPTER 2: REASON FOR THE TRIBULATION IS OPPOSITE THE REASON FOR THE RAPTURE

- Tribulation Defined
- Church Age Ends, Trials and Judgment Begin
- The OT Book of Daniel Provides the Basis for the Tribulation
- Daniel 9:24: "The Key to All End Times Prophecy"
- 70 Weeks Determined
- 1. The Going Forth of the Commandment to Restore and Build Jerusalem
- 2. Unto Messiah the Prince: Jesus
- 3. Messiah "Cut Off": Jesus Rejected
- God's "Prophetic Time Clock" Stopped
- Jews Dispersed and Later Re-Gathered to Israel
- 7 Years Remain to be Fulfilled
- The Tribulation is to "Finish the Transgression..."
- Reason for the Rapture is Opposite the Reason for the Tribulation
- Believers Not Appointed to Wrath
- The Church is the Lord's Bride--And His Body

The reason for the Rapture is the opposite of the reason for the Tribulation. During the Tribulation God will again be dealing personally with His chosen people, the Jews, 144,000 of whom will be commissioned to spread the Gospel of Salvation since the Church has been raptured. The Rapture is for the Church—both current Jew and Gentile believers in Lord Jesus.

Tribulation Defined

The Tribulation period is a time of testing and judgment when God once again begins dealing personally with His people Israel, like He did in the Old Testament. He will seal with His Holy Spirit 144,000 from all the tribes of Israel and these will preach the Gospel of Redemption via Jesus Christ [Rev. 7:3-4], while God also holds the recalcitrant accountable for rejecting the Messiah/Jesus.

As previously stated, the Tribulation is a time of wrath. Currently Satan's and man's wrath are being held in check by the Holy Spirit, as Paul states in 2 Thessalonians 2:7:

"For the mystery of iniquity doth already work: only he who now letteth will let, until he be taken out of the way."

Most Bible scholars believe the restrainer ("he who now letteth") is the Holy Spirit holding back the "mystery" or secret power of lawlessness which will be revealed in the form of the anti-Christ, which is discussed further in CHAPTERS 3 AND 6. Currently, God's Holy Spirit also resides within the followers of the Lord Jesus—and they will be taken out of the way; that is: raptured.

Church Age Ends, Trials and Judgment Begin

The 7-year Tribulation Period is in distinct contrast to our current dispensational age, termed the Church Age or Age of Grace--a near 2,000 year period that began with Christ's resurrection--where judgment for sin is not being imputed due to Jesus' work on the cross. This Age will end when the Lord Jesus "catches up" His followers in the Rapture to keep them from the hour (the Tribulation) that will try the whole earth [Rev. 3:10] as well as the Lord's people Israel:

Zechariah 13:8,9: "And it shall come to pass, that in all the land, saith the LORD, two parts therein shall be cut off and die; but the third shall be left therein. And I will bring the third part through the fire, and will refine them as silver is refined, and will try them as gold is tried: they shall call on my name, and I will hear them: I will say, It is my people: and they shall say, The LORD is my God."

The OT Book of Daniel Provides the Basis for the Tribulation

The OT Book of Daniel explains the reasons for the Tribulation. Daniel was a devout Jewish man, one of the captives in Babylon after Nebuchadnezzar's invading army destroyed Jerusalem and Solomon's Temple. God allowed His people to be taken captive because they had gone astray, led by debauched leaders (Kings and priests). Israel was engaging in even more sinful behavior than the nations surrounding them when they were supposed to be a light to the world and lead people to God. God had warned them many times that their behavior would lead to chastisement with their captivity in Babylon, and that this captivity would last for 70 years [Jeremiah 25:11].

Israel had been in the land since Joshua led them into it for 490 years (70 weeks of years). In addition to their going astray, the Israelites had never let the land rest (Sabbath) as God commanded, but kept planting and harvesting.

Daniel had been reading Scripture and he was aware that the 70 years of captivity in Babylon were about to come to an end. He was godly; cared for his people Israel, and prayed fervently, pouring out his heart to God pleading on their behalf. God honored that, so He sent his personal angel, Gabriel, to give Daniel wisdom and guidance as seen beginning with Daniel Chapter 9 v. 20-23:

20 "And whiles I was speaking, and praying, and confessing my sin and the sin of my people Israel, and presenting my supplication before the LORD my God for the holy mountain of my God"

21 "Yea, whiles I was speaking in prayer, even the man Gabriel, whom I had seen in the vision at the beginning, being caused to fly swiftly, touched me about the time of the evening oblation."

22 "And he informed me, and talked with me, and said, O Daniel, I am now come forth to give thee skill and understanding."

23 "At the beginning of thy supplications the commandment came forth, and I am come to shew thee; for thou art greatly beloved: therefore understand the matter, and consider the vision."

Daniel 9:24: "The Key to All End Times Prophecy"

Gabriel had come to give Daniel a prophetic overview of events that Israel as a nation would experience over ensuing centuries. The most important event being the very day the Messiah--Jesus--would arrive in Israel. That is why Chapter 9 of Daniel verse 24 onward is termed by Biblical scholars as "The Key to All End Times Prophecy."

70 Weeks Determined

Gabriel went on to say in verse 24:

"Seventy weeks are determined upon thy people and upon thy holy city, to finish the transgression, and to make an end of sins, and to make reconciliation for iniquity, and to bring in everlasting righteousness, and to seal up the vision and prophecy, and to anoint the most Holy."

One "week" of 7 years is a Hebrew "heptad," like our decade is 10 years long. So, 70 weeks adds up to 490 years. In verses 25 and 26 Gabriel states:

*"Know therefore and understand, that from **1.** The going forth of the commandment to restore and to build Jerusalem **2.** Unto the Messiah the Prince shall be seven weeks, and threescore and two weeks…the street shall be built again, and the wall, even in troublous times. And after **3.** Threescore and two weeks shall Messiah be cut off,* but not for himself: and the people of the prince that shall come shall destroy the city and the sanctuary; and the end thereof shall be with a flood, and unto the end of the war desolations are determined."*

1. The Going Forth of the Commandment to Restore and Build Jerusalem

God's "Prophetic time Clock" began "ticking" when the commandment to "restore and build Jerusalem" was issued. Most Bible scholars believe the command was issued by the Medo-Persian ruler Artaxerxes and point to Nehemiah 2:1 *"In the month of Nisan in the twentieth year of King*

Artaxerxes..." Other scholars believe it was Cyrus who issued the command per Ezra 1:2 *"Thus saith Cyrus king of Persia, The LORD God of heaven hath given me all the kingdoms of the earth; and he hath charged me to build him an house at Jerusalem, which is in Judah."* Most agree that the command was issued in 445 BC.

2. Unto Messiah the Prince: Jesus

The "*seven weeks and threescore and two weeks*" add up to 69 weeks or 483 years of the 70 weeks determined. Gabriel was telling Daniel exactly when the Messiah would appear.

Just as scholars debate as to the exact day the command to restore and build Jerusalem was issued, they also debate the date when the 483 years of the 490 determined ended. Some believe it was the day Jesus was crucified; others believe it was the very day the Lord Jesus rode into Jerusalem and allowed Himself to be declared King. This happened on 14 April in the year 32. This was such an important day that if the Lord's disciples didn't declare His Kingship, the very rocks would have cried out [Luke 19:40]. The Messiah's entrance into Jerusalem was also prophesied in Zechariah 9:9:

"Rejoice greatly, O daughter of Zion; shout, O daughter of Jerusalem: behold, thy King cometh unto thee: he is just, and having salvation; lowly, and riding upon an ass, and upon a colt the foal of an ass."

3. Messiah "Cut Off": Jesus Rejected

"...threescore and two weeks shall Messiah be cut off, but not for himself..."

Jesus' rightful Kingship was rejected by his people who said "We will not have this man reign over us" per Luke 19:14.

Prior to His crucifixion Jesus mourned over the spiritual blindness of His people, saying in Luke 13:34:

"O Jerusalem, Jerusalem, which killest the prophets, and stonest them that are sent unto thee;

how often would I have gathered thy children together, as a hen doth gather her brood under her wings, and ye would not!"

The Lord's people did not discern the "signs of the times" [Matt. 16:3]. Israel was looking for a conquering King riding a white horse who would restore the glory of their kingdom as it was under David or Solomon. But without a change in their sinful nature--without being born-again by God's Holy Spirit--even a nation at its pinnacle would inevitably denigrate into sin and debauchery as Israel had many times in the past, and as modern nations have in more recent history.

(*NOTE: The first 7 weeks is the time period when the city was being rebuilt and the remaining 62 weeks covers the time when the walls around Jerusalem were rebuilt.)

God's "Prophetic Time Clock" Stopped

Either on the day Jesus rode into Jerusalem, or at the time of His crucifixion, God's "Prophetic Time Clock" stopped ticking.

Jews Dispersed and Later Re-gathered to Israel. In 70 AD the armies of Roman Emperor Titus destroyed Herod's Temple, as foretold to Daniel by the angel Gabriel: *"and the people of the prince that shall come shall destroy the city and the sanctuary"* (Dan. 9:26-27). Jesus foretold this in Matthew 24 after He departed from the temple and His disciples wanted to show Him the lovely buildings around it:

"See ye not all these things? Verily I say unto you, There shall not be left here one stone upon another, that shall not be thrown down."

After destruction of the temple the Diaspora began where Jews left Israel for all parts of the globe. Since then there had been an approximate 2,000-year interval when God didn't seem to be dealing with Israel; that is, until 1948 when Israel was miraculously re-established as a sovereign nation. The relationship to Israel being re-established to God's Prophetic Time Clock, the Rapture, and the Tribulation is discussed further in CHAPTER 3 "Israel and Daniel's 70th Week."

7 Years Remain to be Fulfilled

The 70th Week--the remaining 7 years of the 490 years--is yet to be fulfilled and this is the 7-Year Tribulation Period. I believe it was Sir Robert Anderson in his work "The Coming Prince" [1] who said that the epoch of the 70th Week begins in the same manner as the start of the 490 years; that is, from the going forth of the commandment to restore and to build Jerusalem. As such, there needs to be a ruler to issue this command. This command will start God's Prophetic Time Clock "ticking" again as it regards the 7 remaining years. This is discussed in more detail in CHAPTER 3.

The Tribulation is to "Finish the Transgression ..."

Dan. 9 v. 24 gives the reason for the Tribulation or 70th Week:

"to finish the transgression, and to make an end of sins, and to make reconciliation for iniquity, and to bring in everlasting righteousness,

and to seal up the vision and prophecy, and to anoint the most Holy."

Reason for the Rapture is Opposite the Reason for the Tribulation

The aforementioned shows that the reason for the Rapture is the opposite of the reason for the Tribulation. The Tribulation is a time when God tries and refines His people Israel, and for judgment of all who have rejected the Salvation of the Lord Jesus (the "transgression of 9:24). Followers of Jesus (both Jew and gentile) have accepted Salvation; as such, the Lord promises to keep them from wrath.

Believers Not Appointed to Wrath. This bears repeating. The apostle Paul tells us:

1 Thess. 5:9 "For the God hath not appointed us to wrath, but to obtain salvation by our Lord Jesus Christ."

Rom. 5:9-11 "Much more then, being now justified by his blood, we shall be saved from wrath through him For if, when we were enemies,

we were reconciled to God by the death of his Son, much more, being reconciled, we shall be saved by his life. And not only so, but we also joy in God through our Lord Jesus Christ, by whom we have now received the atonement."

Dr. Gerald Stanton expounds upon this, stating that people who argue for a post-tribulation rapture don't understand that the Tribulation doesn't deal with the Church, but with Israel and its purification:

"The Tribulation concerns Daniel's people the coming of 'false Messiahs,' the preaching the gospel of the kingdom, flight on the Sabbath, the Temple and Holy place; the land of Judea, the city of Jerusalem, the twelve tribes of the Children is Israel; the song of Moses, the covenant with the Beast; the sanctuary sacrifice and the oblation of the Temple ritual. These all speak of Israel and clearly demonstrate that the Tribulation is largely a time of God's dealing with His ancient people prior to their entrance into the promised kingdom..."[2].

The Church is the Lord's Bride—And His Body

The Church as the Bride of Christ is taught throughout Scripture. Christ's relationship to His church is allegorical to the marriage between a man and woman. Paul in his epistle to the Ephesians 5:23-33 touches on this, and in 2 Corinthians 11 Paul refers to the Church there as being espoused to Christ:

"For I am jealous over you with godly jealousy: for I have espoused you to one husband, that I may present you as a chaste virgin to Christ."

The Church is also the body of Christ as Paul states in Romans 12:5

"So we, being many, are one body in Christ, and every one members one of another."

This sheds light on God's comment in Genesis 2:24:

"Therefore shall a man leave his father and his mother, and shall cleave unto his wife: and they shall be one flesh."

In 1 Corinthians 12:27 Paul states:

"Now ye are the body of Christ, and members in particular."

The Church as the Body of Christ is pre-figured in Genesis where God fashioned Eve from Adam's body--his rib--and she became Adam's bride. Jesus is the "new" or last Adam [1 Cor. 15:45] who had His side pierced on the cross.

Therefore, the Church is Jesus' bride and as such He, as a loving husband, will protect His Bride from Tribulation.

WORKS CITED & SCRIPTURE REFERENCED IN CHAPTER 2

[1] **Sir Robert Anderson.** The Coming Prince: The Marvelous Prophecy of Daniel's Seventy Weeks Concerning the Antichrist, Published by Cosimo Classics (December 1, 2007)

[2] **Dr. Gerald Stanton.** Archived on Rapture Ready
http://www.raptureready.com/resource/stanton/gerald_stanton.html/

Rev. 7:3-4 Saying, Hurt not the earth, neither the sea, nor the trees, till we have sealed the servants of our God in their foreheads. And I heard the number of them which were sealed: and there were sealed an hundred and forty and four thousand of all the tribes of the children of Israel.

Rev. 3:10 Because thou hast kept the word of my patience, I also will keep thee from the hour of temptation, which shall come upon all the world, to try them that dwell upon the earth.

Jer. 25:11 And this whole land shall be a desolation, *and* an astonishment; and these nations shall serve the king of Babylon seventy years.

Luke 19:40 And he answered and said unto them, I tell you that, if these should hold their peace, the stones would immediately cry out.

Luke 19:14 But his citizens hated him, and sent a message after him, saying, We will not have this man to reign over us.

Matt. 16:3 And in the morning, It will be foul weather to day: for the sky is red and lowring. O ye hypocrites, ye can discern the face of the sky; but can ye not discern the signs of the times?

Ephes. 5:23-32 For the husband is the head of the wife, even as Christ is the head of the church: and he is the saviour of the body. Therefore as the church is subject unto Christ, so *let* the wives *be* to their own husbands in every thing. Husbands, love your wives, even as Christ also loved the church, and gave himself for it; That he might present it to himself a glorious church, not having spot, or wrinkle, or any such thing; but that it should be holy and without blemish. For no man ever yet hated his own flesh; but nourisheth and cherisheth it, even as the Lord the church: This is a great mystery: but I speak concerning Christ and the church.

1 Cor. 15:45 And so it is written, The first man Adam was made a living soul; the last Adam *was made* a quickening spirit.

CHAPTER 3: ISRAEL AND DANIEL'S 70TH WEEK

- Salvation From the Jews and To the Jew First
- 70th Week Distinctly Jewish in Nature
- Approximate 2,000 Year Interval Between diaspora and 1948
- The Coming One Week Covenant: the Remaining 7 Years
- Psalm 83 War and the Commandment to "Restore and Build Jerusalem"
- Start of the 70th Week: Covenant with Anti-Christ
- First 3 1/2 Years of Tribulation Fairly Peaceful
- Mid-Week: Anti-Christ Breaks the Covenant
- Last 3 1/2 Years: "Time of Jacob's Troubles"
- End of the Tribulation: Christ's 2nd Advent
- 3 Signs of the Imminent Rapture
- Parable of the Fig Tree

Salvation From the Jews and To the Jew First

The apostle Paul, a Hebrew of the Hebrews, wrote that salvation is to the Jew first:

Romans 1:16 "For I am not ashamed of the gospel of Christ: for it is the power of God unto salvation to everyone that believeth; to the Jew first, and also to the Greek."

Rom. 2:9,10 "Tribulation and anguish, upon every soul of man that doeth evil, of the Jew first, and also of the Gentile; but glory, honour, and peace, to every man that worketh good, to the Jew first, and also to the Gentile"

Gentiles who believe in the Lord Jesus have the Jews to thank. From them came the Messiah, Jesus. Paul also wrote in Romans that God has not cast away his people whom he fore chose…and if by their casting away equals the reconciling of the world then the receiving of them would be "life from the dead" [Rom. 11:1-15]. In this epistle Paul cautions Gentiles against boasting of their salvation since they are branches grafted into a wild olive tree [Rom. 11: 16-24].

Paul states in Romans 11:25-27:

"For I would not, brethren, that ye should be ignorant of this mystery, lest ye should be wise in your own conceits; that blindness in part is happened to Israel, until the fullness of the Gentiles be come in. And so all Israel shall be saved: as it is written, There shall come out of Sion the Deliverer, and shall turn away ungodliness

from Jacob: For this is my covenant unto them, when I shall take away their sins."

God has big plans for Israel, to bring them into His Kingdom. As such it is incumbent upon those who have obtained salvation to intercede for them and "Pray for the peace of Jerusalem" per Psalm 122:6-9:

"Pray for the peace of Jerusalem: they shall prosper that love thee. Peace be within thy walls, and prosperity within thy palaces. For my brethren and companions' sakes, I will now say, Peace be within thee. Because of the house of the LORD our God I will seek thy good."

God said of Abraham and his offspring in Genesis 12:1-4:

"[I] will... make of thee a great nation, and I will bless thee, and make thy name great; and thou shalt be a blessing: And I will bless them that bless thee, and curse him that curseth thee: and in thee shall all families of the earth be blessed."

Gentiles are forever indebted to the Jewish people. Nonetheless, the Tribulation--Daniel's 70th Week--is to try and refine God's people Israel. This is another proof of a Pre-Tribulation Rapture.

70TH Week Distinctly Jewish in Nature

Daniel tells us that the Tribulation, or 70th Week, is distinctly Jewish in nature and that it has nothing to do with the Church. Verses 9:26-27 shed prophetic light on the history and future of Israel and the coming 7-Year Tribulation:

"and the people of the prince that shall come shall destroy the city and the sanctuary; and the end thereof shall be with a flood, and unto the end of the war desolations are determined."

This is a double or "near and far" prophecy. The people of the prince that shall come refers to the world-governing Roman empire during Jesus' time on earth (which was Gentile at the time, not "European") as well as the one-world empire ("Beast") during the Tribulation [Rev. 13], which also will be Gentile in make-up and not just "European."

Approximate 2,000 Year Interval Between Diaspora and 1948

After the Jewish Temple was destroyed there occurred the Diaspora--the scattering of Jews throughout nations of the globe. Eventually, Israel ceased from being a nation. That is until 1948 when Israel was miraculously reestablished as a sovereign nation against all odds, while fighting bigger, better equipped armies, as prophesied in Ezekiel 37:1-12:

"The hand of the LORD was upon me...and set me down in...the valley which was full of bones...O ye dry bones, hear the word of the LORD...Behold I will cause breath to enter into you, and ye shall live...and behold...the bones came together...the sinews and flesh came upon them...Thus saith the Lord GOD; Come from the four wind, O breath, and breath upon these slain...these bones are the whole house of Israel...I will open your graves, and cause you to come up out of your graves, and bring you into the land of Israel."

In addition Daniel 12:1 states:

"And at that time shall Michael stand up, the great prince which standeth for the children of thy people: and there shall be a time of trouble, such as never was since there was a nation even to that same time..."

The Coming One Week Covenant: the Remaining 7 Years

Daniel 9:27 says that when Israel is once again a nation some ruler will confirm a "covenant" with them (and the rest of the world probably):

"And he shall confirm the covenant with many for one week: and in the midst of the week he shall cause the sacrifice and the oblation to cease, and for the overspreading of abominations he shall make it desolate, even until the consummation, and that determined shall be poured upon the desolate."

This covenant for "one week" is the 70th Week, the remaining 7 years, or the 7-Year Tribulation period.

Psalm 83 War and the Commandment to "Restore and Build Jerusalem"

Israel is now again in existence as a sovereign nation and Jerusalem is its Capital. What could happen on the world scene that would necessitate the restoration and building of Jerusalem? At this time nearly all of Israel's surrounding neighbors want to eliminate them from being a nation, and many people who follow events occurring in the Middle East believe these nations will try to make good on their threats against Israel.

Many Biblical scholars believer a war will soon break out between Israel and her surrounding neighbors, Muslim nations who want to see Israel wiped off the map. Scholars believe that this war is the one prophesied in Psalm 83. In verse 6-8 of this prophetic Psalm Israel's current neighbors are named:

"The tabernacles of Edom, and the Ishmaelites; of Moab, and the Hagarenes; 7 Gebal, and Ammon, and Amalek; the Philistines with the inhabitants of Tyre; 8 Assur also is joined with them..."

In verse 4 the Psalm explains how the neighbors of Israel feel about them today:

"They have said, Come, and let us cut them off from being a nation; that the name of Israel may be no more in remembrance. For they have consulted together with one consent: they are confederate against thee:"

In verse 18 the Psalmist pleads for their destruction by the Lord: *"That men may know that thou, whose name alone is JEHOVAH, art the most high over all the earth."*

The last verse with God's name in capitals is to show the Muslim enemies of Israel that God's name is *not* Allah but JEHOVA.

While God will no doubt fight on behalf of His people during this war, it will—as all wars do—bring destruction and chaos. A world leader who is expert at diplomacy will need to "come on the scene to help broker a "peace" and settle the chaos.

It is during the Psalm 83 war that the probability of an errant missile launched by one of

Israel's enemies could destroy the Muslim Dome of the Rock near the Jewish Temple Mount. This would provide impetus to allow the Jews to build their Temple; that is, after a covenant is made "to restore and build Jerusalem" as Dan. 9:27 states. This will begin the 70th Week or 7-Year Tribulation.

Start of the 70th Week: Covenant with Anti-Christ

The anti-Christ of Revelation 6 is the "he" of Daniel 9:27. This man is first presented as a diplomatic conqueror in Revelation 6:2 as there are no arrows in his bow, but he is shown wearing a crown signifying his authority. Initially he shows himself to be a friend of Israel. He is the one who signs the covenant of Daniel 9:25:

"Know therefore and understand, that from the going forth of the commandment to restore and to build Jerusalem…"

This world-figure, in addition to signing the covenant with Israel, unifies all the nations of the world and forms the one-world government, or Beast of Revelation Chapter 13. This needs to happen for at least two reasons:

1) the Psalm 83 war has wreaked havoc on Israel and wiped out most of Israel's enemies;

2) right before or after this saw the disappearance (Rapture) of 2 billion of the world's peoples who were followers of Jesus.

First 3 1/2 Years of Tribulation Fairly Peaceful

The first half of the Tribulation week will most likely be fairly peaceful. This is primarily because the diplomatic conqueror of Revelation 6 sets up the one-world government and Israel is allowed to build their Temple and restore Jerusalem. Also, it is Satan's modus operandi to subtly ensnare people by deceit using his ability to appear as an "angel of light" per Paul in 2 Corinthians 11:14:

"And no marvel; for Satan himself is transformed into an angel of light."

Eventually people are inextricably ensnared in his grasp.

Mid-Week: Anti-Christ Breaks the Covenant

Daniel 9:27 tells us that in the middle of the 7-Years --after 3 1/2 years, or Mid-Week--the man who confirmed the covenant with Israel will go back on his word. "a*nd in the midst of the week he shall cause the sacrifice and the oblation to cease"*

Here is where the one-time friend of Israel is revealed as the anti-Christ when he sets himself up in the Temple and claims himself to be God, per Revelation 13. In verse 3 of this chapter John writes:

"And I saw one of his heads as it were wounded to death; and his deadly wound was healed: and all the world wondered after the beast."

It has been speculated that after this once-friend of Israel claims in the Temple that he is God someone assassinates him, hence the "deadly wound." It is at this point that Satan likely enters him bodily and he is "revived."

Last 3 1/2 Years: "Time of Jacob's Troubles"

From mid-Week onward the 70th Week is known as "The Time of Jacob's Troubles" [Jer. 30:7], Jacob being the patriarch of the 12 tribes, God having changed his name to Israel. The anti-Christ will now severely persecute Israel as explained in Revelation, and finally within this scenario occurs the Battle of Armageddon, when people amass to fight against the Lord Himself as Revelation 16:16 attests:

"And he gathered them together into a place called in the Hebrew tongue Armageddon."

End of the Tribulation: Christ's 2nd Advent.

After the Tribulation the Lord Jesus returns to earth with His followers (whom He raptured beforehand) to rule and reign, as Revelation 19:14-16 attests:

"And the armies which were in heaven followed him upon white horses, clothed in fine linen, white and clean. And out of his mouth goeth a sharp sword, that with it he should smite the nations: and he shall rule them with a rod of iron: and he treadeth the winepress of the fierceness and wrath of Almighty God. And he hath on his vesture and on his thigh a name written, KING OF KINGS, AND LORD OF LORDS.

3 Signs of the Imminent Rapture

Since the 7-Year Tribulation, or 70th Week, is distinctly Jewish in most aspects, there are three prophetic sign posts that point to the imminence of the Rapture:

1. 1948--Israel a Sovereign Nation Once Again.
2. Jerusalem in Israel's Hands. Jerusalem was captured in the Six Day War in 1967.
3. Plans to Build the Temple have been in the making for several years now.

Parable of the Fig Tree

The Fig tree is symbolic of Israel as a nation, and in Matthew 24:32 Jesus explains:

"Now learn a parable of the fig tree; When his branch is yet tender, and putteth forth leaves, ye know that summer is nigh:..."

With this parable Jesus is saying that when Israel puts forth leaves then it is near the time when all the signs of the imminent 70th Week as well as the Rapture are in place. The 3rd Temple will be built in Jerusalem upon the signing of the Covenant with anti-Christ.

This Chapter showed that the Tribulation Period is actually Daniel's 70th Week and is distinctly Jewish in nature, which points to a Pre-Tribulation Rapture for Jesus' Church.

SCRIPTURE REFERENCED IN CHAPTER 3

Rom. 11:1-15 I say then, Hath God cast away his people? God forbid..... God hath not cast away his people which he foreknew. .... Even so then at this present time also there is a remnant according to the election of grace.... I say then, Have they stumbled that they should fall? God forbid: but *rather* through their fall salvation *is come* unto the Gentiles, for to provoke them to jealousy. Now if the fall of them *be* the riches of the world, and the diminishing of them the riches of the Gentiles; how much more their fullness?... For if the casting away of them *be* the reconciling of the world, what *shall* the receiving *of them be*, but life from the dead?

Rom. 11:16-24 For if the firstfruit *be* holy, the lump *is* also *holy*: and if the root *be* holy, so *are* the branches. And if some of the branches be broken off, and thou, being a wild olive tree, wert graffed in among them, and with them partakest of the root and fatness of the olive tree; Boast not against the branches. But if thou boast, thou bearest not the root, but the root thee. Thou wilt say then, The branches were broken off, that I might be graffed in. Well; because of unbelief they were broken off, and thou standest by faith. Be not highminded, but fear:...And they also, if they abide not still in unbelief, shall be graffed in: for God is able to graff them in again. For if thou wert cut out of the olive tree which is wild by nature, and wert graffed contrary to nature into a good olive tree: how much more shall these, which be the natural *branches*, be graffed into their own olive tree?

Rev. 13:1-5 And I stood upon the sand of the sea, and saw a beast rise up out of the sea, having seven heads and ten horns, and upon his horns ten crowns, and upon his heads the name of blasphemy. And the beast which I saw was like unto a leopard, and his feet were as the feet of a bear, and his mouth as the mouth of a lion: and the dragon gave him his power, and his seat, and great authority. And I saw one of his heads as it were wounded to death; and his deadly wound was healed: and all the world wondered after the beast. And they worshipped the dragon which gave power unto the beast: and they worshipped the beast, saying, Who is like unto the beast? who is able to make war with him? And there was given unto him a mouth speaking great things and blasphemies; and power was given unto him to continue forty and two months.

Rev. 6:2 And I saw, and behold a white horse: and he that sat on him had a bow; and a crown was given unto him: and he went forth conquering, and to conquer.

Jer. 30:7: Alas! for that day *is* great, so that none *is* like it: it *is* even the time of Jacob's trouble; but he shall be saved out of it.

CHAPTER 4: RAPTURES AND PRE-FIGURES OF SUCH IN THE OLD AND NEW TESTAMENTS

- Old Testament Raptures and Pre-Figures of the Pre-Tribulation Rapture
- Enoch Raptured
- Noah & Family Delivered
- Lot & His 2 Daughters Delivered
- Rahab & Family Delivered
- Elijah Raptured
- Isaiah: Pre-Tribulation Rapture for Saint's Protections
- Zechariah: After Tribulation Raptured Return to Earth
- New Testament Records Several Individuals Raptured
- Jesus Raptured at Ascension; Paul and John Raptured; Lord's Two Witnesses Raptured at End of Their Witness
- Gospels Speak of Calling Up/Away of Christ's Followers; Matthew 24:37; Matthew 25: Parable of 10 Virgins; Luke 21:36
- Why John's Gospel Omits Olivet Discourse
- Epistles Speak of Pre-Tribulation Rapture
- Paul's Epistles; Peter's Epistle; John's Epistle; Jude's Epistle
- Raptures & Saving From Judgment Indicate Begin/End of Dispensations
- Book of Revelation: Much Evidence for Pre-Tribulation Rapture

As mentioned in CHAPTER 1 the Rapture is not a new doctrine. The Old Testament contains record of people having been raptured, as well as several people saved out of judgment as pre-figures of a Pre-Tribulation Rapture. The New Testament also bears record of several individuals who have been raptured, or "called up" to Heaven by God.

Old Testament Raptures and Pre-Figures of the Pre-Tribulation Rapture

Genesis describes memorable instances where people are raptured or saved out of judgment because of their belief in God's promises and His faithfulness. Enoch was raptured and Noah and his family, and Lot and his daughters are the individuals who were delivered because they "believed God" and it was accounted to them as righteousness [Galatians 3:6]. As such they also were not appointed to wrath or judgment.

Enoch Raptured

In Genesis 5:24 the brief story of Enoch's life is told: *"And Enoch walked with God and was not, for God took him."* Enoch lived on the cusp of the Noachian Flood wherein after his rapture, the whole violent, corrupt world would be destroyed. He didn't have "religion"; he didn't have "the law"; Jesus had not yet died on the cross for his sins—but Enoch knew of the plan of salvation [Gen. 3:15], believed God's promise, and more than likely ruminated over it as it as the world was further denigrating into the chaos of violence. This is similar to believers today who are awaiting the Rapture.

Noah & Family Delivered

Noah and his family were saved out of the Flood, which destroyed the whole world [Gen. 7:7].

Lot & His 2 Daughters Delivered

Genesis 19 speaks of these three being saved out of Sodom and Gomorrah which were destroyed in judgment. Lot's wife looked back, probably not wanting this to happen or maybe in disbelief that it would happen, and as such she was turned into a pillar of salt.

Rahab & Family Delivered

In the book of Joshua these individuals were saved by Joshua and his men from the destruction of the corrupt nation-city Jericho because of Rahab's belief in the mighty power of the Hebrew God [Joshua 6:23]. This speaks of a Pre-Tribulation Rapture as *Joshua* is a form of *Yehoshuah*, which is an alternate form of Yeshua, which is Jesus' name in Hebrew. Yeshua in Hebrew is a verb derived from "to rescue" and "to deliver"[1]. So in this instance Joshua is a pre-figure of Jesus who will deliver/rapture His followers.

Elijah Raptured

In 2 Kings Chapter 2 v. 11 Elijah is raptured; that is, taken up to Heaven. Elijah prophesied during the time of Israel's corrupt kings and priests who led their people astray to do worse than the nations around them, including engaging in the practice of child sacrifice. Elijah warned Israel that it would be overcome by the Assyrians.

Isaiah: Pre-Tribulation Rapture for Saint's Protection

In Chapter 26 v. 19-20 the Rapture is alluded to as a protection/removal/hiding "behind doors" (see Rev. 4:10) of God's people until "the indignation be overpassed." Then in v. 21 the prophet tells us *"The Lord cometh out of His place to punish the inhabitants of the earth for their iniquity."* Since believers are "saved from wrath" this speaks of the Pre-Tribulation Rapture.

Zechariah: After Tribulation Raptured Return to Earth

This book is termed by Biblical scholars "The Little Revelation." Its prophecies tell of what happens to Jerusalem in the last days. In Chapter 14 v. 5 Zechariah states *"...and the Lord my God shall come, and all the saints with thee"* in the context of events at the very end of the Tribulation. This speaks for a Pre-Tribulation Rapture.

New Testament Records Several Individuals Raptured

Jesus, Paul, John, and the two Witnesses in Revelation Chapter 11 are examples of individuals having been raptured.

Jesus Raptured at Ascension

This is recorded in the NT book of Acts 1:19:

"And when he had spoken these things, while they beheld, he was taken up; and a cloud received him out of their sight."

This occurred at the start of a new dispensation; that is, the Church Age/Age of Grace. Jesus will rapture His followers at the end of this dispensation, before the Tribulation.

Paul and John Raptured

Paul explained in his epistle to the Corinthians about his rapture:

2 Cor. 12:2 "I knew a man in Christ above fourteen years ago, (whether in the body, I cannot tell; or whether out of the body, I cannot tell: God knoweth;) such an one caught up to the third heaven."

12:4 "How that he was caught up into paradise, and heard unspeakable words, which it is not lawful for a man to utter."

John in Revelation Chapter 4:1-3 is raptured:

"After this I looked, and, behold, a door was opened in heaven: and the first voice which I heard was as it were of a trumpet talking with me; which said, Come up hither, and I will shew thee things which must be hereafter..."

Lord's Two Witnesses Raptured at End of Their Witness

In Revelation Chapter 11:11, 12 it is shown that the Lord's two Witnesses whom He sent to earth are raptured after their mission of witnessing of Salvation via the Lord Jesus is done:

"And after three days and an half the Spirit of life from God entered into them, and they stood upon their feet; and great fear fell upon them which saw them. And they heard a great voice from heaven saying unto them, **Come up hither**. *And they ascended up to heaven in a cloud; and their enemies beheld them."*

Gospels Speak of the Calling Up/Away of Christ's Followers

In the Gospels several passages speak of the Rapture of Jesus' followers.

The Olivet Discourse (OD)

In the OD recorded in Matthew. 24, Mark 13 and Luke 21, the Lord Jesus while speaking upon the Mount of Olives just outside Jerusalem tells His disciples--who are Jewish--some of the things that will happen to His people around the end of the age. Not coincidentally the Mount of Olives is the very place where the Lord will set His feet when He returns to the earth at the 2nd Advent with all his saints following Him, per Zechariah 14:4-5:

"And his feet shall stand in that day upon the Mount of Olives, which is before Jerusalem on the east..."

Matthew 24:37

Here the Lord likens the end times leading up to the Rapture and the Tribulation as "the days of Noah." No one would heed Noah's warning that the whole world would be destroyed with a flood. Noah was saved out of the flood judgment because he lived righteously, believed God, and took action. Noah is a type/figure of today's believers.

In Chapter 24 Jesus mentions twice that people will be taken to heaven at His coming, while at this same instance others will be left behind. In verse 40 onward:

"Then two shall be in the field; the one shall be taken and the other left. Two women shall be grinding at the mill; the one shall be taken and the other left. Watch therefore: for ye know not what you're your Lord doth come."

The aforementioned was an example of His coming for His followers only.

Some argue that "taken" refers to "taken for judgment" but this does not fit the context. If this were after the Tribulation the Lord would not admonish anyone to "watch."

Matthew 25: Parable of 10 Virgins

Here, the Lord continues His theme of two different types of people and where they will spend the Tribulation period. From the context we see that Jesus is contrasting His followers with those who take no thought of the "signs of the times" and were not "watching." The "signs" refer to pre-Tribulation occurrences as does the word "watching," because during the Tribulation there are no signs and people don't need to "watch"--they need to try to survive.

The Lord starts this parable with the phrase *"Then shall the kingdom of heaven be likened unto..."* not "People in the Tribulation will be like this..." From v. 1 to v. 13 the Lord talks of 5 wise and 5 foolish virgins. The wise ones had oil in their lamps. This oil is symbolic of spiritual insight that comes from having the Holy Spirit and from reading Scripture. As such, these five are able to navigate their way through dark streets/dark times, and were watching for the Lord's appearing. The other five had no oil in their lamps. By the time these unwise virgins did finally purchase oil for their lamps it was too late: the Lord had already in v. 10 shut the door on them. This door is the one John sees in Revelation 4 when he is called up to Heaven.

Ending this parable in v. 13 the Lord Jesus states *"Watch therefore, for ye know neither the day nor the hour wherein the Son of man cometh."* Here the Lord cannot be speaking of His 2nd Advent at the end of the Tribulation because everyone will know that 7 years is 7 years. Also, in Revelation it states that people aren't happy to see Him at the end of the Tribulation.

It is interesting to note that in this parable the Lord Jesus speaks of 10 virgins. Why did He not simply say "Here's a story of two types of peoples"? Ten (10) is the number symbolic of Gentiles in Scripture. In Genesis 10 Noah's son Japheth is the father of all Gentile nations. These are the Gentile nations seen in Ezekiel 38 that describes the war of Gog and Magog which many scholars believe will occur during the Tribulation

Period symbolized by the red horse in Rev. 6:4. (See CHAPTER 6 for more on Ezek. 38.)

Revelation 10:7 states:

"But in the days of the voice of the seventh angel, when he shall begin to sound, the mystery of God should be finished, as he hath declared to his servants the prophets"

The mystery of God is that salvation would be offered to the Gentiles [Colossians 1:27]. It is probably not coincidental that the statement regarding the fact that salvation to the Gentiles will be finished is in Revelation Chapter 10. Again, ten (10) is the number in Scripture that refers to Gentiles. The number 7 signifies completion.

With the parable of the 10 virgins the Lord is referring to the fact Gentiles mainly accepted his Lordship while collectedly His people did not. And during these last days most of the church is Gentile. Some will be wise (reading Scripture, doing His commands) and some foolish, not having the oil of spiritual insight in their lamps. (Interestingly the parable ends on v 13 and in Revelation 13 we see the rise of the Gentile Beast, or one-world government.)

Luke 21:36

Here the Lord urges his disciples to *"Watch therefore and pray always that you may be accounted worthy to escape all these things that shall come to pass."* He is speaking of things that occur during the Tribulation. He states also that *"this generation shall not pass until all be fulfilled"* [Mark 13:30; Luke 21:32]. "All" here means the things John writes about in Revelation.

Why John's Gospel Omits Olivet Discourse

John's Gospel doesn't contain the OD. I believe this is another proof of a Pre-Tribulation Rapture. John instead is given the Revelation by the Lord Himself. John was the "beloved disciple" who was very spiritually in-tuned with the Lord's mindset. The Lord entrusted the care of His mom Miriam [John 19:27] to John. In the Revelation

John is given details of the things only touched upon in the synoptic Gospels. In Revelation John is symbolic of all Pre-Tribulation believers who have been raptured. (More on that in CHAPTER 5.)

Epistles Speak of Pre-Tribulation Rapture

Paul, Peter, John and Jude speak of the Pre-Tribulation Rapture.

Paul's Epistles

The many instances where Paul talks of the Rapture have already been cited in this work, but some bear repeating here:

1 Cor. 15: 51-54: *"Behold, I shew you a mystery; We shall not all sleep, but we shall all be changed, In a moment, in the twinkling of an eye, at the last trump: for the trumpet shall sound, and the dead shall be raised incorruptible, and we shall be changed."*

1 Thess. 2:19: "For what is our hope, or joy, or crown of rejoicing? Are not even ye in the presence of our Lord Jesus Christ at his coming?"

1 Thess. 5:5 "And the very God of peace sanctify you wholly; and I pray God your whole spirit and soul and body be preserved blameless unto the coming of our Lord Jesus Christ."

Paul expounds upon this in 1 Thessalonians 4:17:

"Then we which are alive and remain shall be caught up together with them in the clouds, to meet the Lord in the air: and so shall be ever be with the Lord."

Scripture does not speak of the Lord's followers being called up to meet the Lord in the clouds at the end of the Tribulation period (or during it, for that matter either). The only mention of an "end of Tribulation Rapture" is the case of the Lord's two Witnesses in Revelation 11.

Peter's Epistle

Peters 2nd epistle in 2:9 states *"The Lord knoweth how to deliver the godly out of temptations, and to reserve the unjust unto the Day of Judgment to be punished."*

1 Peter 1:7: "That the trial of your faith, being much more precious than of gold that perisheth, thought it be tried with fire, might be found unto praise and honour and glory at the appearing of Jesus Christ."

1 Pet. 1:13: "Wherefore gird up the loins of your mind, be sober, and hope to the end for the grace that is to be brought unto you at the revelation of Jesus Christ."

John's Epistle

John informs us that when Jesus appears (at the Rapture) we will be like Him:

1 John 3:2: "Beloved, now we are the sons of God, and it doth not yet appear what we shall be: but we know that, when he shall appear, we shall be like him: for we shall see him as he is."

Jude's Epistle

Jude mentions Enoch, the seventh from Adam who was taken up to Heaven by God. Jude states that Enoch prophesied of the ungodly saying

"the Lord will return to earth with ten thousands of his saints"

These saints return to judge the ungodly. They saints need to return to earth from somewhere, and that somewhere is Heaven where they were kept safe throughout the 7-Year Tribulation period. This speaks clearly for a Pre-Tribulation Rapture.

Raptures & Saving From Judgment Indicate Begin / End of Dispensations

Scripture records the rapture of several people, as previously shown, as well as the deliverance/saving out of judgment of several people, also discussed previously. The common thread in all these events is that they signal either the end of a dispensational era or the beginning of one.

Enoch in Genesis was raptured before the world-wide judgment of the Flood. Noah and his family was delivered from this judgment to begin a new era in humanity.

Lot and his daughters were delivered just after the start of the new covenants God made with Abraham. In Genesis 17:15 God changed Abram's name to Abraham; instituted the covenant of circumcision (17:10); changed Sarai's name to Sarah (17:15); confirmed the establishment of His covenant to bring Jesus/Messiah via Isaac (17:19).

Shortly thereafter the large nation-cities in the vast plain near Abraham and Lot were destroyed. This is a pre-figure of the whole world being judged. In fact, it appeared to Lot's daughters that the whole world was destroyed, per Genesis 19:31 *"...there is not a man in the earth..."*

Rahab and her family in the book of Joshua were delivered as a new era in Israel's history was beginning. Joshua Chapter 5 records events right before Israel enters the Promised Land after wandering 40 years in the wilderness (so the older, un-believing generation could die off); the manna from Heaven had ceased and they now ate of the "fruit of the land of Canaan" (5:12). This was the beginning of a new dispensational era.

It is interesting to note the parallel of the trumpet call of the Lord's voice in Revelation to the fact that the Israelites in destroying the corrupt nation-city of Jericho blew trumpets and compassed the city seven times.

In 2 Kings Elijah was raptured as Israel was about to get a new king, Jehu (19:16); Syria a new king: Hazael (19:15); Elisha would be the prophet in Elijah's stead (19:16); and eventually Israel would be overcome by Assyrians.

Zechariah Chapter 14 speaks of the Lord returning to earth with His raptured followers. In verses 2 and 3 of Chapter 14 he describes the events of Revelation19:17:

"For I will gather all nations against Jerusalem to battle... Then shall the Lord go forth and fight against those nations."

In verses 4 and 5 Zechariah prophesies of how the Lord will return to earth with his followers:

" And his feet shall stand in that day upon the mount of Olives, which is before Jerusalem... ...and the Lord my God shall come, and all the saints with thee..."

This speaks of a new dispensation, which is Jesus Millennial Reign on earth.

The rapture/Ascension of the Lord Himself speaks of the new dispensation for it signals the end of the Law of Moses and the beginning of the Age of Grace/Church Age.

The rapture of the two Witnesses in Revelation 11 speaks of the ending of one dispensation—the Tribulation—as Revelation 11 is parenthetical with Revelation 18. This is just before the new dispensation of the Lord's Millennial Reign.

All of the above examples of either people having been raptured or saved out of judgment signal either the beginning of a new dispensational type/ era, or the ending of one.

These are proofs of a Pre-Tribulation Rapture as the Rapture event itself speaks of the end of the Church Age and the beginning of the Tribulation Period.

Book of Revelation: Much Evidence for Pre-Tribulation Rapture

There are so many evidences for a Pre-Tribulation Rapture in the book of Revelation that the next two CHAPTERS of this book are reserved for that discussion.

WORKS CITED & SCRIPTURE REFERENCED IN CHAPTER 4

[1] **Wikipedia.** Yeshua (ישוע, with vowel pointing יֵשׁוּעַ – yēšūăʿ in Hebrew) was a common alternative form of the name יְהוֹשֻׁעַ ("Yehoshuah" – Joshua) in later books of the Hebrew Bible and among Jews of the Second Temple period. Meaning "salvation" in Hebrew, it was also the most common form of the name Jesus hence the name corresponds to the Greek spelling Iesous, from which, through the Latin Iesus, comes the English spelling Jesus. Main article: Names and titles of Jesus in the New Testament Yeshua in Hebrew is a verbal derivative from "to rescue", "to deliver"
https://en.wikipedia.org/wiki/Yeshua_%28name%29

Gal. 3:6 Even as Abraham believed God, and it was accounted to him for righteousness.

Gen. 3:15 5 And I will put enmity between thee and the woman, and between thy seed and her seed; it shall bruise thy head, and thou shalt bruise his heel.

Gen. 7:7 And Noah went in, and his sons, and his wife, and his sons' wives with him, into the ark, because of the waters of the flood.

Josh. 6:23 And the young men that were spies went in, and brought out Rahab, and her father, and her mother, and her brethren, and all that she had; and they brought out all her kindred, and left them without the camp of Israel.

2 Kings 2:11 And it came to pass, as they still went on, and talked, that, behold, there appeared a chariot of fire, and horses of fire, and parted them both asunder; and Elijah went up by a whirlwind into heaven.

Matt. 25 Then shall the kingdom of heaven be likened unto ten virgins, which took their lamps, and went forth to meet the bridegroom. And five of them were wise, and five were foolish. They that were foolish took their lamps, and took no oil with them: But the wise took oil in their vessels with their lamps. While the bridegroom tarried, they all slumbered and slept. And at midnight there was a cry made, Behold, the bridegroom cometh; go ye out to meet him. Then all those virgins arose, and trimmed their lamps. And the foolish said unto the wise, Give us of your oil; for our lamps are gone out. But the wise answered, saying, Not so; lest there be not enough for us and you: but go ye rather to them that sell, and buy for yourselves. And while they went to buy, the bridegroom came; and they that were ready went in with him to the marriage: and the door was shut. Afterward came also the other virgins, saying, Lord, Lord, open to us. But he answered and said, Verily I say unto you, I know you not. Watch therefore, for ye know neither the day nor the hour wherein the Son of man cometh.

Coloss. 1:27 To whom God would make known what is the riches of the glory of this mystery among the Gentiles; which is Christ in you, the hope of glory:

Mark 13:30 Verily I say unto you, that this generation shall not pass, till all these things be done.

Luke 21:32 Verily I say unto you, This generation shall not pass away, till all be fulfilled.

Jude 1:14-15 And Enoch also, the seventh from Adam, prophesied of these, saying, Behold, the Lord cometh with ten thousands of his saints, To execute judgment upon all, and to convince all that are ungodly among them of all their ungodly deeds which they have ungodly committed, and of all their hard speeches which ungodly sinners have spoken against him.

John 19:27 Then saith he to the disciple, Behold thy mother! And from that hour that disciple took her unto his own home.

CHAPTER 5: THE BOOK OF REVELATION PROVIDES MOST EVIDENCE FOR A PRE-TRIB RAPTURE

- Specific Statements Point to Pre-Tribulation Rapture
- "The Lord's Day" in Chapter 1
- Jesus Promises to Keep Followers from Tribulation 86
- Parenthetical Structure of 6-18: Church Not Mentioned Throughout
- Divisions of the Book
- Chapter 19 "And after these things"
- Chapters 1,2 & 3: Change of Speakers / Locale
- Chapter 12: All About Israel
- Chapter 16--Problematic?
- Reason for Tribulation: Big Proof of Pre-Tribulation Rapture
- The 144,000 Witnesses of Revelation 7 are Jewish
- The 144,000 are Martyred for Their Testimony of Jesus
- Chapter 19: The Church is Christ's Heavenly bride Who Returns to Earth with Him

The Book of Revelation—or more properly The Revelation of Jesus Christ--is itself the replete with evidence for a pre-Tribulation Rapture. It is the only book in the Bible that promises a special blessing for reading and "keeping" the things within it [Rev. 1:3]. "Keeping" means not twisting the words or saying that it is all merely symbolic in terms of it not describing specific peoples, locals or events, when its symbolism does just that. In fact Revelation is so rife with symbolism that speaks of a Pre-Tribulation Rapture that CHAPTER 6 of this book is devoted exclusively to discussing it.

This CHAPTER'S discussion on the evidence for a Pre-Tribulation Rapture centers on the following:

1. Specific Statements for a Rapture—including the Lord's own words;

2. The fact that Chapters 6-18--which describe events within the 70th Week -- never speak of the Church;

3. The book's division into different sections via key phrases, each signaling a change of location and "dispensations," among other evidences.

Specific Statements Point to Pre-Tribulation Rapture

Several statements, including many made by the Lord Himself, prove a Pre-Tribulation Rapture.

"The Lord's Day" in Chapter 1

At the beginning of Revelation John is on earth, the isle of Patmos, when the Lord speaks to him as shown in v. 1:10-11:

"I was in the Spirit on the Lord's day, and heard behind me a great voice, as of a trumpet, Saying, I am Alpha and Omega, the first and the last: and, What thou seest, write in a book..."

John hears the Speaker, but doesn't see Him. This changes at Revelation 4:1-3 where John sees the Speaker because he is bodily called up to Heaven (raptured):

"After this I looked, and, behold, a door was opened in heaven: and the first voice which I heard was as it were of a trumpet talking with me; which said, **Come up hither,** *and I will shew thee things which must be hereafter..."*

As previously mentioned this call *to "Come up hither"* is the trumpet Voice the Lord's followers will hear when they are raptured.

Jesus Promises to Keep Followers from Tribulation

In Revelation 3:10 Jesus addresses the Philadelphian church, promising to keep them from tribulation:

"Because thou has kept the word of my patience, I also will keep thee from the hour of temptation which shall come upon all the world to try them that dwell upon the earth."

"The hour" is the Tribulation. Compare this hour with the "about a half hour" of Revelation 8:1 where there is *"silence in heaven for about a half hour."* This half hour is the last half of the Tribulation. Chapter 8 is "parenthetical" with 15; that is, 7 chapters apart within the narrative, but they should be read in sequence: 8 then 15. These chapters cover the events that take place in last half or 3 1/2 years of the 7 year Tribulation Period.

In Chapter 2 the Lord promised to "keep" His followers in the Philadelphia-type church from tribulation. In contrast He warns those in the Thyatira-type church that unless they repent he *"...will cast them into great tribulation."*

Parenthetical Structure of 6-18: Church Not Mentioned Throughout

I believe it was Sir Robert Anderson in his work "The Coming Prince" [1] who first pointed out that Revelation Chapters 6 through 18 were "parenthetical" within the narrative; that is, they are 7 chapters apart from one another. In other words read Chapter 6 then read Chapter 13; read Chapter 7 then Chapter 14 all the way through to 18. This does not, however, hold true for Chapter 12—which is all about the Nation of Israel, and which weaves into the 7 year Tribulation period at verse 6. This parenthetical structure is significant because within these Chapters—the Tribulation Narrative—all events during the Tribulation are described, yet not once does the Lord Jesus address

His Church. This proves that the Church is not on earth during the Tribulation.

The "Parenthetical" structure of Chapters 6-18 can be illustrated on a graphic for a better visual:

7 Year Tribulation

1	2	3	4	5	6	7
Start		**Mid-Week**				**End**
Chap. 6	Chap. 7	Chap. 8	Chap. 9	Chap. 10	Chap. 11	
Chap. 13	Chap. 14	Chap. 15	Chap.16	Chap. 17	Chap. 18	

It should be noted that 1) Chapters 6 & 13 run throughout the 7 years; 2) After Mid-Week--the last 3 1/2 years of the Tribulation--the Lord Himself shortens the days; therefore, events happen very rapidly from that point onward.

Again, throughout the 7-Year period covered in Chapters 6-18 the Lord never once addresses His church. The reason for this is because the reason for the Tribulation is opposite the reason for the Rapture as previously explained. In Revelation Chapters 1-4 it is shown that the Holy Spirit speaks to individuals and the churches during the Church Age. The phrase *"After this"* in Revelation 4 indicates God's Spirit is not speaking to the Church.

This silence extends through the Tribulation period. There can only be one reason for this: all of Christ's pre-Tribulation followers are resident in Heaven with Him.

There is never an instance in Scripture where God won't address His sincere followers. There is plenty of evidence that He stops speaking to the recalcitrant, as evidenced by the 400 "silent" years that intervened from the end of the OT book of Malachi to the announcement of the birth of the Messiah in the Gospels. Ray Stedman gives a detailed account of these years in his work "The Silent Years: The 400 Years Between the Old and New Testaments" [2].

Divisions of the Book

The late pastor of Calvary Chapel, Chuck Smith, stated that there are three distinct divisions of time/place in Revelation, those being "things which thou has seen, and the things which are, and the things which shall be hereafter" and that after the Lord's address to the 7 churches ("things that are") and the term "After this" denotes new sections or dispensations:

"So after the things that pertain to the church we read 'After this I looked, and, behold, a door was opened in heaven: and the first voice which I heard was as it were of a trumpet talking with me; which said, Come up hither, and I will shew thee things which must be hereafter.'"

"'After this' John writes 'Immediately I was in the spirit: and, behold, a throne was set in heaven (4:2).' Here is the demarcation where John, symbolic of the entire church is called up before the Tribulation. Note that the saints sing a song before the Lord who is seen as a lamb that was slain. Then they sang a new song saying 'Thou art worthy to take the book, and to open the seals thereof: for thou wast slain, and hast <u>redeemed</u> us to God by thy blood out of every kindred, and tongue, and people, and nation... (Rev. 5:7-10)."

It is worth noting that the song to the Lord is sung by the "redeemed"—Christians and Messianic Jews. Smith points out that the lyrics are only those that the church can sing:

"If we follow the timing, we see that the church singing the song...occurs in chapter 5 before the opening of the scroll in chapter 6, and that proceeds the tribulation on earth..." [3].

Chapter 19 "And after these things"

In this Chapter, the 70TH Week has run its course. The phrase "*And after these things*" signifies a new division which is the end of the Tribulation, and the end of the parenthetical structure of the narrative that ran from Chapter 6 through Chapter 18. This verse indicates a significant change in time and place as it regards where the Lord's followers are. In Chapter 4 they are in Heaven prior to the Tribulation giving glory to the Lord. In 19:1 They're still there giving glory to the Lord but in preparation will return to earth with Him in His 2nd Advent.

There actually appears to be four divisions in Revelation:

Revelation 4:1 "***After this*** *I looked, and, behold, a door was opened in heaven: and the first voice which I heard was as it were of a trumpet talking with me; which said, Come up hither, and I will shew thee things which must be hereafter.*"

John, symbolic of the Church, has been raptured. (More on this symbolism in CHAPTER 6.)

Revelation 7:1 "*And **after these things** I saw four angels standing on the four corners of the earth, holding the four winds of the earth, that the wind should not blow on the earth, nor on the sea, nor on any tree.*"

Prior to this time in Revelation Chapter 6, six of the seven seals were opened on the Scroll (the 7th seal is opened in Revelation Chapter 8). This chapter signifies a new dispensation: Jews exclusively are sealed with God's Spirit and they are the witnesses commissioned to spread the Gospel.

Revelation 18:1 "*And **after these things** I saw another angel come down from heaven,* *having great power; and the earth was lightened with his glory."*

End of the Tribulation.

Revelation 19 :1 *"And **after these things** I heard a great voice of much people in heaven, saying, Alleluia; Salvation, and glory, and honour, and power, unto the Lord our God:"*

Right before Christ's 2nd Advent.

Only Revelation Chapter 4 has the phrase "After this," the others have "After these things." The "After this" in 4 means after the Church Age/Age of Grace. The other phrases speak of events in/after the Tribulation period. This is subtle, but it is another proof of a Pre-Tribulation Rapture.

Chapters 1, 2 & 3: Change of Speakers/ Locale

A subtle wording in Revelation 1-3 is also notable in that it indicates a change of speakers and locale. In v. 3 it is the "Lord's angel" speaking to

John while he is still on earth, versus the Lord Himself speaking to John which happens in verse 4, because at this time John is in Heaven, a pre-figure of the Pre-Tribulation Rapture.

Also in Chapters 2 and 3 it is first *the Lord's angel* who is to write to the 7 churches and John is named as the "bishop" of these. Then there is the big change in locale and Who is speaking to John in Revelation 4, which is *Jesus Himself.* This is to show that John, who is symbolic of the Church, is there in Heaven "After this" when the Church Age is over.

Chapter 12: All About Israel

This Chapter is all about the Nation of Israel and it stands alone outside the Tribulation narrative until verse 6. Verse 5 is reference to the Lord Jesus/Messiah:

"And she [Israel] *brought forth a man child* [Jesus], *who was to rule all nations with a rod of iron, and her child was caught up unto God, and to his throne."*

This is a reference to Jesus Himself being raptured to God at His Ascension recorded in Acts 1:9:

"And when he had spoken these things, while they beheld, he was taken up; and a cloud received him out of their sight."

From verse 5 in Chapter 12 to verse 6 there is a near 2,000 year period of time when God essentially stopped dealing with His people Israel on a national basis. This is the dispensation known as the Church Age/Age of Grace. The fact verse 6 of Chapter 12 weaves into the Tribulation narrative when it does is another proof of a Pre-Tribulation Rapture as it shows a change in dispensations, from the Church Age to the Tribulation.

Verse 6 of Revelation 12 weaves into the parenthetical structure of Revelation Chapters 6-18 during Mid-Week:

"And the woman [Israel] fled into the wilderness, where she hath a place prepared of God, that they should feed her there a thousand two hundred and threescore days."

One thousand two hundred and sixty days equals 3 1/2 years. At this point in the 70th Week the anti-Christ, who first portrayed himself as Israel's "friend" and diplomatic conqueror in Revelation 6:2...:

"And I saw, and behold a white horse: and he that sat on him had a bow; and a crown was given unto him: and he went forth conquering, and to conquer."

...is now at this Mid-Week point in Revelation 13:5-7 Israel's great enemy:

"And there was given unto him a mouth speaking great things and blasphemies; and power was given unto him to continue forty and two months. And he opened his mouth in blasphemy against God, to blaspheme his name, and his tabernacle, and them that dwell in heaven. And it was given unto him to make war with the saints, and to overcome them: and power was given him over all kindreds, and tongues, and nations."

It is important to keep in mind that the narrative in Revelation 13 runs throughout the 7 Year Tribulation.

As far as the anti-Christ at Mid-Week being Israel's great enemy: Jesus warned His people of this in John 5:43:

"I am come in my Father's name, and ye receive me not: if another shall come in his own name, him ye will receive."

Chapter 16--Problematic?

Some hold up Revelation 16:15 as problematic with the Pre-Tribulation Rapture belief because here Jesus says *"Behold I come as a thief. Blessed is he that watched and kept his garments."* This chapter has described events that occur right before the very end of the Tribulation period, before the "great and terrible day of the Lord" [Joel 2:31], or The Battle of Armageddon [Rev. 16:16-18].

The difficulty can be cleared up by showing this is an interjection into the narrative warning to those to not get this far to where they need to go through the Tribulation. Revelation 16 is parenthetical with Revelation 9. As shown previously in the small graphic it is important to remember that things happen real fast near the end since the Lord has shortened the days as Matthew 24:22 attests:

"And except those days should be shortened, there should no flesh be saved: but for the elect's sake those days shall be shortened."

Therefore, since the Lord interjects this statement near the end of the Tribulation it would make no sense for Him to rapture his followers at this point because it certainly wouldn't mean that He kept them from Tribulation. In other words, there would be no need for rapture at this point.

Notes to the online King James Version (KJV) of the Bible offer both *Wesley's* and the *People's Bible Notes* for Revelation 16:15. Both concur that Revelation 16:15 is an interjection or warning. [4]

Reason for Tribulation: Big Proof of Pre-Tribulation Rapture

The reason for the 7-Year Tribulation, or 70th Week of Daniel, is directed at the nation of Israel. This is in itself is big proof of a pre-Tribulation Rapture. Dr. Gerald Stanton so aptly states the 70th Week:

"...is the 'Time of Jacob's Troubles,' not the 'Time of the Church's Troubles.' This gives us the reason that the Lord Jesus does not address His church during the Tribulation period covered in Rev. Chapters 6 through 18."[5]

Stanton says that during this time Satan is shown as angry against Israel who flees to a place in the wilderness where God had prepared her a refuge from the serpent of Rev. 12:13-16, explaining:

"If in that same day, the Church, the very body of Christ, were on the earth, how much more would she be the object of Satan's attack! How great would his havoc be, for Revelation records no place of refuge for the Church during the days

the Tribulation. Fortunately, she will be in heaven, removed from Satan's wiles (Rev. 12:9)."

The 144,000 Witnesses of Revelation 7 are Jewish

Currently the Lord's Church--both Jew and Gentile members--are commissioned to spread the Gospel of Salvation by Jesus Christ. During the 70th Week, this task is given exclusively to Jews from the 12 tribes of Israel whom God seals with His Holy Spirit [Rev. 7:3 onward]. Dan and Ephraim are not mentioned because they were the first tribes to fall into idolatry [Judges 18:30; Hosea-4:17], so symbolically God doesn't name them.

The 144k sealed Jews are those who will preach the Gospel during the 70th Week since this is the time Daniel 9:24 speaks of.

The 144,000 are Martyred for Their Testimony of Jesus

After these witnesses to the Gospel of Salvation are martyred there is no human being on earth with God's Holy Spirit, so God sends and angel to fly through the atmosphere preaching the Gospel [Rev. 14:6].

Dr. Stanton points out that God's judgment during the Tribulation also falls upon Gentile nations that have rejected Jesus, saying:

"The 'cities of the nations' shall fall, after which Satan shall be bound 'that he should deceive the nations no more, till the thousand years should be fulfilled (Rev. 20:30)."

"God's judgment falls likewise upon the individual wicked, the kings of the earth, the great, the rich, and the mighty, every bondman and every free man (Rev 6:15-17). It falls upon all who blaspheme the name of God and repent not to give Him glory (Rev. 16:9). Wicked men, godless nations, suffering Israel—these may all be found in Revelation 6-18; but one looks in vain for the church of Christ, which is His body, until he reaches the nineteenth chapter..."

Chapter 19: The Church is Christ's Heavenly Bride Who Returns to Earth with Him

Stanton wraps it up:

"There [the Church] is seen as the heavenly bride of Christ, and when He returns to earth to make His enemies His footstool, she is seen returning with Him."

WORK CITED & SCRIPTURE REFERENCED IN CHAPTER 5

[1] **Sir Robert Anderson,** The Coming Prince: The Marvelous Prophecy of Daniel's Seventy Weeks Concerning the Antichrist, Published by Cosimo Classics (December 1, 2007)

[2] **Ray C. Stedman**, The Silent Years: THE 400 YEARS BETWEEN THE OLD AND NEW TESTAMENTS
http://ldolphin.org/daniel/silentyears.html

[3] **Pastor Chuck Smith**, The Rapture of the Church, Through The Bible C2000 Series on The Word For Today
http://www.thewordfortoday.org

[4] **Wesley's and People's Notes on Rev. 16:15.**
The Bible, KJV
http://www.kingjamesbibleonline.org/

[5]**Gerald Stanton**
http://www.raptureforums.com/GeraldStanton/stanton2.cfm.

Rev. 1:3 Blessed is he that readeth, and they that hear the words of this prophecy, and keep those things which are written therein: for the time is at hand.

Joel 2:31 The sun shall be turned into darkness, and the moon into blood, before the great and the terrible day of the LORD come.

Rev. 16:16-18 And he gathered them together into a place called in the Hebrew tongue Armageddon. And the seventh angel poured out his vial into the air; and there came a great voice out of the temple of heaven, from the throne, saying, It is done. And there were voices, and thunders, and lightnings;

and there was a great earthquake, such as was not since men were upon the earth, so mighty an earthquake, and so great.

Rev. 7:3 onward... Saying, Hurt not the earth, neither the sea, nor the trees, till we have sealed the servants of our God in their foreheads. And I heard the number of them which were sealed: *and there were* sealed an hundred *and* forty *and* four thousand of all the tribes of the children of Israel.

Judg. 18:30 And the children of Dan set up the graven image: and Jonathan, the son of Gershom, the son of Manasseh, he and his sons were priests to the tribe of Dan until the day of the captivity of the land. And they set them up Micah's graven image, which he made, all the time that the house of God was in Shiloh.

Hosea 4:17   Ephraim is joined to idols: let him alone.

Rev. 14:6 And I saw another angel fly in the midst of heaven, having the everlasting gospel to preach unto them that dwell on the earth, and to every nation, and kindred, and tongue, and people,

CHAPTER 6: SYMBOLISM IN THE BOOK OF REVELATION PROVES THE PRE TRIB RAPTURE

- John Symbolic of all Believers
- 7 Spirits are Complete Work of Holy Spirit in the Church; 7 Churches Symbolize Complete Church Age; 24 Elders Symbolize All the Redeemed
- Old Testament Pre-Figure of 24 Elders
- The Beast of Revelation Chapter 13 is Entire Un-Redeemed World
- Conglomerate of Daniel's Beasts; Satan is Behind the Beast; The Beast is Scarlet--Symbolic of Sin
- Anti-Christ is "Little Horn" per Daniel
- God's Beast Around Throne Counter to World's Beast
- Martyrs of Revelation 7:9 Clothed in White
- John a Pre-Trib Believer Doesn't Recognize Martyrs
- God's Wrath Finally Poured Out
- "It is Done": No Post-Tribulation Rapture
- Mystery Babylon: Confusion
- Believers Think Opposite of Mystery Babylon
- Symbolic Harlot: False Religion of Sacrifice
- Mystery Babylon The Great: Worldly Commercial System
- That Great City: Jerusalem
- Symbolic Sodom and Egypt
- The Hour that Will Try the Whole World

The book of Revelation is rife with symbolism that proves the Pre-Tribulation Rapture. To discern the meaning of its symbols it is necessary to compare symbolism with symbolism while comparing Scripture with Scripture.

John Symbolic of All Believers

John is Bishop of the 7 Churches in Revelation 3 and 4, and no doubt started many of them. John's was the only Gospel that omitted the Olivet Discourse because Jesus gave His beloved disciple greater detail with the Book of Revelation. When John began following Jesus he was called one of the sons of Thunder [Mark 3:17] ready to call fire down upon unbelievers, but his heart was changed from one of judgment to love. This alludes to the change in dispensational eras of judgment under the OT law, to grace during the Church age. During the Tribulation the Church Age has ended and the 70th Week has begun. John is in Heaven throughout this time period.

It was shown in CHAPTER 5 that the change of speakers and locale in Revelation Chapters 1, 2 & 3 indicate John is first on earth, then raptured to Heaven. Also pointed out was the subtle change in wording where first the Lord's angel is to write to the 7 churches, then in Revelation 4 it is the Lord

Himself who is speaking to John showing that he is in Heaven when the "Church Age" is over.

The 7 Spirits are Complete Work of Holy Spirit in the Church

The number 7 is consistently used throughout Scripture as the number of completion. Genesis tells us that God rested on the 7th day because all of His works of creation were complete. In Revelation 1 the 7 spirits are a complete Holy Spirit's work with the Church. As with the Tribulation: it is 7 years long, signifying the completion of the reasons for the Tribulation as mentioned in the earlier discussion of the end-times prophecies in the book of Daniel.

7 Churches Symbolize Complete Church Age

The 7 churches in Revelation Chapters 3 and 4 symbolize the completion of the dispensational era known as the "Church Age" or "Age of Grace" where God's judgment for sin in not imputed due to Christ's work on the Cross. Chapters 3 added to 4 equals 7.

This Church Age has lasted for about 2,000 years. Peter in 2 Peter 3:8 explains:

"But, beloved, be not ignorant of this one thing, that one day is with the Lord as a thousand years, and a thousand years as one day."

He also states in 2 Pet. 3:9:

"The Lord is not slack concerning his promises as other men count slackness but is longsuffering toward usward wishing that none should perish but all come to repentance."

This Church Age will end when as Paul puts it in Romans 11:25 "the fullness of the gentiles be come in":

"For I would not, brethren, that ye should be ignorant of this mystery, lest ye should be wise in your own conceits; that blindness in part is happened to Israel, until the fulness of the Gentiles be come in."

After all the Gentiles are redeemed by Jesus then God will begin dealing personally again with His people Israel.

24 Elders Symbolize All the Redeemed

All the redeemed prior to the start of the 70th Week are symbolized by the 24 Elders around God's Throne in Revelation 4:

"And round about the throne were four and twenty seats: and upon the seats I saw four and twenty elders sitting, clothed in white raiment; and they had on their heads crowns of gold."

The 24 Elders first mentioned here are clothed in white with crowns of gold on their heads. These are all who believed in Jesus as their Savior and are now in Heaven with their glorified bodies having been raptured.

These Elders are not mentioned from Revelation Chapter 5 until Chapter 11. Chapter 11 is parenthetical with Chapter 18, so this is at the end of the Tribulation period. Sometimes what God leaves out is important. What God has left out is that these Elders, symbolizing the pre-Tribulation redeemed, are not addressed—like the Church is not addressed—until the end of the Tribulation period.

Old Testament Pre-Figure of 24 Elders

The Old Testament contains a symbolic pre-figure of the 24 Elders of Revelation. Since the 24 Elders are "symbolic" it helps to look for other "symbolic" references, and we find this in Genesis 24. Twenty four is the symbolic addition of the 12 Tribes of Israel that sprang from faith of Abraham plus the 12 Apostles in the NT. In Genesis Chapter 24 Abraham is a "type" or "figure" of God the Father. Isaac is a type of Jesus as Abraham's son. Abraham's un-named Servant is a type of Holy Spirit who is commanded to find a bride, Rebekah (symbolic of the Church) for Abraham's son Isaac. This un-named Servant never testifies of Himself, but only of Isaac, just like the Holy Spirit never testifies of Himself, only about things of the Lord Jesus, as John 16:13-15 states:

"Howbeit when he, the Spirit of truth, is come, he will guide you into all truth: for he shall not speak of himself; but whatsoever he shall hear, [that] shall he speak: and he will shew you things to come. He shall glorify me: for he shall receive of mine, and shall shew [it] unto you. All things that

the Father hath are mine: therefore said I, that he shall take of mine, and shall shew [it] unto you."

The un-named Servant is only to bring Rebekah, symbolic of the Church (the Lord's Bride), if she is willing. And the Servant is not to look outside Israel to unbelievers or Canaanites.

Abraham was of faith before the law (of Moses) was instituted. Because Abraham believed God's promises he was accounted by God as righteous (Gal. 3:6), just like Church Age believers are. Christians today are not under the Law of Moses. Jesus fulfilled the law by dying for our sins on the cross and His Holy Spirit imparts into us His Nature so when we walk with God obeying Him we (super)naturally fulfill the law. This is where God's nation Israel collectively went astray: they thought they were righteous because they had the law, but they rejected Jesus.

Another scholar whose work I read years ago--and whose name all those years ago I neglected to write down--pointed out that other elements of Scripture attest to the 24 Elders being all believers:

"...you will note that parenthetical Chapters 6-18 give us 12 such chapters, yet Chapter 12 which is all about Israel is an exception. Now look at Rev 12:12. It totals 24. The number '12' is written all over New Jerusalem, and there are 24 elders in Heaven after the Rapture in Rev. 4:1. Now look at Rev. 12:12 which states 'Rejoice then, O heaven and you that dwell therein! But woe to you, O earth and sea, for the devil has come down to you in great wrath, because he knows that his time is short!'"

Having said that it begs the question: who else would be dwelling in heaven but the Lord's believers symbolized as the 24 Elders? Also, the witnesses to Christ during the 70th Week are all Jewish, and after they have been martyred there is no one else to proclaim the Gospel so God commissions an angel to fly in the atmosphere to do this for the poor deluded souls left on earth, as shown in Revelation 14:6:

"And I saw another angel fly in the midst of heaven, having the everlasting gospel to preach unto them that dwell on the earth, and to every nation, and kindred, and tongue, and people..."

Only at the end of the Tribulation does Revelation mention the 24 Elders again (Rev. 11:16, which is parenthetical with Chapter 18). These are not mentioned throughout the Tribulation narrative where disaster upon disaster occurs on earth, first through man's inhumanity to man, then Satan's wrath, then finally God's judgments toward the unrepentant.

Perhaps most importantly is that at the end of the Tribulation Period the Lord Jesus does not call His followers up to meet with Him in the air; rather, His followers come with Him to earth as previously cited.

The Beast of Revelation Chapter 13 is Entire Un-Redeemed World

This Beast of Revelation 13 from its origin of having been formed from "the sea" (meaning sea of peoples/people of the world, Rev. 17:15) at the very start of the Tribulation represents the entire un-believing world.

Rev. 13:1-5: "*And I stood upon the sand of the sea, and saw a beast rise up out of the sea, having seven heads and ten horns, and upon his horns ten crowns, and upon his heads the name of blasphemy. And the beast which I saw was like unto a leopard, and his feet were as the feet of a bear, and his mouth as the mouth of a lion: and the dragon gave him power, and his seat, and great authority. And I saw one of his heads as it were wounded to death; and his deadly would was healed: <u>and all the world wondered after the beast</u>. And they worshipped the dragon which gave power unto the beast: and they worshipped the beast, saying, Who is like unto the beast? who is able to make war with him? And there was given unto him a mouth speaking great things and blasphemies; and power was given unto him to continue forty and two months.*"

Revelation 13:3 states that the whole unredeemed world "wondered" (followed) after this system of government as the solution to the chaos that preceded its formation (the Psalm 83 war; the Rapture of Jesus' followers, economic chaos, etc.).

The Beast is the entire Godless one-world socio-political-economic governing system. After all, all of Jesus' followers have been raptured.

Parts of this Revelation Beast can be seen in the Daniel Chapters 2 and 7. Daniel sees the coming empires of Babylon, Medo-Persia and Greece as beasts or animals whose characteristics symbolize the characteristics of the empires they represent. The Lion symbolized Nebuchadnezzar's Babylon the first known world-ruling empire; the Bear represented the Medo-Persian Empire; the Leopard symbolized the Grecian empire.

Conglomerate of Daniel's Beasts

In Revelation 13 John sees these beasts of Daniel 7 as a conglomeration into one Beast, for it has characteristics of all three of Daniel's (Dan. 7:4-6):

Mouth=Lion. Strong, prideful creature who essentially has no enemies. Also symbolizes arrogance / self-sufficiency and no need for God, as Babylon's Nebuchadnezzar thought of himself.

Body=Leopard. Symbolizing the "body politic" or "Democracy." Like ancient Greece it will be autocratic.

Feet = Feet of Bear indicates this one-world government springs up rapidly—most likely after the Rapture. The Medo-Persian Empire rapidly overtook the Babylonian empire.

In addition to having animal characteristics, the Rev. 13 Beast has other attributes:

7 Mountains = Complete Worldly Governments on top of the "arrogant" mouth of the Lion. (Not coincidentally there are 7 mountains around Israel, including the Temple Mount.)

10 Horns = Ruling Strength. On top of the mountains or ruling governments.

10 Crowns = Sovereignty of the 10-nation states.

This Beast will be a 10 nation confederacy as symbolized by the 10 Horns and Crowns atop the horns. It will cover the whole world. It will be not merely "European" in structure as some believe. For that to happen the current EU will need to shed over a dozen member countries—which it may do; however, the Beast will indeed be a global system. The Roman Empire during John's time was not

"European"—it was just Gentile in nature. So the 10 nation Beast that functions during the Tribulation Period is the entire un-redeemed world.

Satan is Behind the Beast

The apostle Paul wrote in Ephesians 6:12:

"For we wrestle not against flesh and blood, but against principalities, against powers, against the rulers of the darkness of this world, against spiritual wickedness in high places."

This wickedness in high places is reference to the satanic power behind the Beast of Revelation 13-2:

"and the dragon gave him his power, and his seat, and great authority."

There are wicked forces behind all human governments (and cultures) that do not have the God of the Bible as their foundation. In the OT these forces are spoken of as *princes* in relation to governments that are against the nation of Israel. The prince of Tyre in Ezekiel 28:1-19 is representative of the Revelation 13 Beast. The prince of Tyre was over the earthly kingdom of Babylon, which is a "type" of Babylon the Great of Revelation 18--the worldly commercial system:

"By thy multitude of they traffic (commerce) they filled the midst of thee with violence..." (Ezek. 28).

The prince of Persia mentioned in Daniel Chapter 10 represents the Medo-Persian Empire (and the thought process behind it); the prince of Grecia represents Western thought. "Gog" (whom I heard but can't confirm is an ancient Syrian word for "darkness") is the chief prince of Meshech and Tubal in Ezekiel 38:2-3:

"Son of man, set thy face against Gog, the land of Magog, the chief prince of Meshech and Tubal, and prophesy against him, and say, Thus saith the Lord GOD; Behold, I am against thee, O Gog, the chief prince of Meshech and Tubal..."

The phrase "Behold I am against thee, O Gog..." means God is against the prince of darkness. During the latter part of the Tribulation Gog leads the coalition of Meshech and Tubal that come against Israel in the latter days, per Ezekiel 38:2, 8 and 9:

"Son of man, set thy face against Gog, the land of Magog, the chief prince of Meshech and Tubal, and prophesy against him...After many days thou shalt be visited: in the latter years thou shalt come into the land that is brought back from the sword, and is gathered out of many people, against the mountains of Israel, which have been always waste: but it is brought forth out of the nations, and they shall dwell safely all of them. ...Thou shalt ascend and come like a storm, thou shalt be like a cloud to cover the land, thou, and all thy bands, and many people with thee."

Michael the archangel is Israel's prince. He fights with Gabriel for Israel against all the above satanic princes (forces) behind worldly governments, per Daniel 10:18-21:

"Then there came again and touched me [one] like the appearance of a man, and he strengthened me, And said, O man greatly beloved, fear not: peace [be] unto thee, be strong, yea, be strong. And when he had spoken unto me, I was strengthened, and said, Let my lord speak; for thou hast strengthened me. Then said he, Knowest thou wherefore I come unto thee? and

now will I return to fight with the prince of Persia: and when I am gone forth, lo, the prince of Grecia shall come. But I will shew thee that which is noted in the scripture of truth: and [there is] none that holdeth with me in these things, but Michael your prince."

In Daniel 2:40-43 the end-times Beast of Revelation 13 is described:

"And the fourth kingdom shall be strong as iron: forasmuch as iron breaketh in pieces and subdueth all things: and as iron that breaketh all these, shall it break in pieces and bruise. And whereas thou sawest the feet and toes, part of potters' clay, and part of iron, the kingdom shall be divided; but there shall be in it of the strength of the iron, forasmuch as thou sawest the iron mixed with miry clay. And as the toes of the feet were part of iron, and part of clay, so the kingdom shall be partly strong, and partly broken. And whereas thou sawest iron mixed with miry clay, they shall mingle themselves with the seed of men: but they shall not cleave one to another, even as iron is not mixed with clay."

In Daniel 7:7 this Revelation 13 Beast is further described:

"After this I saw in the night visions, and behold a fourth beast, dreadful and terrible, and strong exceedingly; and it had great iron teeth: it devoured and brake in pieces, and stamped the residue with the feet of it: and it was diverse from all the beasts that were before it; and it had ten horns."

Nothing stands in the way of the one-world empire Beast of Revelation 13--not even once sovereign world powers.

The Beast is Scarlet--Symbolic of Sin

Revelation 17:3 states:

"...and I saw a woman sit upon a scarlet coloured beast, full of names of blasphemy, having seven heads and ten horns."

Scarlet is the color that in Scripture symbolizes sin, as Isaiah 1:18 attests:

"Come now, and let us reason together, saith the Lord; though your sins be as scarlet, they shall be as white as snow; though they be red like crimson, they shall be as wool."

Here with the scarlet Beast of Revelation 13 we see the great contrast between the white garments of the righteous around God's throne in Heaven. This scarlet Beast shows that there are no Pre-Tribulation followers of the Lord Jesus left on earth at the time of its rise in Revelation 13, which is parenthetical with Revelation 6—which is the start of the 7 year Tribulation.

Going back to the telling phrase in Revelation 13:1-5 *"and all the world wondered after the beast":* followers of Jesus wouldn't follow after this government, so the phrase "all the world" denotes their being in Heaven with the Lord.

Additionally, it was mentioned in CHAPTER 1 that this Beast can't arise until *"he who now letteth will let, until he be taken out of the way"* per Paul in 2 Thessalonians 2:7. He who letteth is the Holy Spirit at work in the world an in followers of Jesus.

Anti-Christ is "Little Horn" per Daniel

The anti-Christ who comes up among the 10 Horns of the Revelation 13 Beast is described as the "little horn" in Daniel 7:8; 7:20:

Dan. 7:8 "I considered the horns, and, behold, there came up among them another little horn, before whom there were three of the first horns plucked up by the roots: and, behold, in this horn were eyes like the eyes of man, and a mouth speaking great things."

Dan. 7:20 "...even of that horn that had eyes, and a mouth that spake very great things, whose look was more stout than his fellows."

Revelation 13 v. 5 says that he has eyes like a man and mouth speaking blasphemies. At Mid-Week Satan had been cast down to earth, as seen in Revelation 9:1:

"...and I saw a star fall from heaven unto the earth: and to him was given the key of the bottomless pit."

"Star" in Scripture is another name for angel; in this case, Satan. He is given the keys to the abyss and out come locusts (demons) to torment only those without God's seal. That would be everyone except the 144,000 Jewish witnesses. Another proof of the Pre-Tribulation Rapture.

Having fallen to earth Satan now in-dwells the once-benevolent conqueror of Revelation 6, then stands in the Temple claiming himself to be God [Rev. 13:1-6], inflaming the Jewish people and apparently 3 of the other "kings" of the 10-nation world-ruling Beast, as can be seen by him "plucking up" 3 of the 10 horns (world powers) in Daniel 7:8. He thus has become the "8th" Cesar-type ruler of Rev. 17:10-11:

"And there are seven kings: five are fallen (Rom. emperors), and one is (during John's time), and the other is not yet come (the anti-Christ, head of the Beast): and when he cometh, he must continue a short space (3 1/2 years): And the beast that was, and is not, even he is the eighth, and is of the seven, and goeth into perdition."

Now (at Mid-Week) the Beast-anti-Christ persecutes the Jewish people, per Daniel 7:21:

"I beheld, and the same horn made war with the saints, and prevailed against them."

The anti-Christ is so incensed he also wants to convince other leaders within the 10-nation confederacy that Mystery Babylon the Great of Revelation 17:5-7 is to be burned with fire (possibly nuclear weapons), as Revelation 17:16 attests:

" And the ten horns which thou sawest upon the beast, these shall hate the whore, and shall make her desolate and naked, and shall eat her flesh, and burn her with fire."

The destruction of Babylon the Great is the culmination of this (Rev. 18) as prophesied in Ezekiel 28:

"...therefore I have cast thee as profane out of the mountain of God (probably the Temple Mount); and I have destroyed thee, O covering cherub, from the midst of the stones of fire. Thine heart was lifted up because of thy beauty, thou has

corrupted thy wisdom by reason of thy brightness...I have cast thee to the ground to earth (Rev. 9) I have laid thee before kings, that they may behold thee (end of Trib., Rev. 18). By the multitude of thine iniquities, in the unrighteousness of thy traffic (commerce), thou has profaned thy sanctuaries; therefore I have brought forth a fire from the midst of thee, it hath devoured thee, and I have turned thee to ashes upon the earth, who have committed fornication and lived deliciously with her (Mystery Babylon), shall bewail her, and lament for her, when they shall see the smoke of her burning, standing afar off for the fear of her torment, saying alas, alas, that great city (Jerusalem, Rev. 11:8)...For in one hour so great riches is come to naught.."

R.A. Torrey, in his work "What the Bible Teaches," says:

"The simplest explanation of all this is that the King of Tyre represents the anti-Christ like the prince of Tyre in the OT was the type of the anti-Christ and that he is to be an incarnation of Satan as the true Christ was an incarnation of God." [1]

God's Beasts Around Throne Counter to the World's Beast

God has counterparts to the Beast of Revelation 13 and these are explicitly shown around His throne:

Rev. 4:7 *"And the first beast was like a lion, and the second beast like a calf, and the third beast had a face as a man, and the fourth beast was like a flying eagle."*

These Beasts (Cherubim) show characteristics of the Lord Jesus as He is portrayed in the four Gospels. This is God's "system" of government, as it were, by redeeming fallen mankind by Jesus Christ. Believers can be reconciled to God and have his very Nature—His Holy Spirit—inside them. (If all humans had the nature of Christ there's be no need for law or governments.)

God's system is unlike the world's system of government—which is inhumane, unequal, cruel, corrupt etc. The world's Beast is completely devoid of God. After all, the followers of Jesus the world over, including Messianic Jews, are no longer on earth. They have been raptured as shown by the fact that God's Beasts are showing John--symbolic of the Church--what is happening on earth in the absence of the Church.

God's Beasts tell John to "Come and see" [Rev. 6:1,3,5 and 7], and they stand with John looking down off the edge of the sea of glass [Rev. 4:6]. Essentially the Beasts are showing us now what is happening in the future, which all of us as followers of Jesus will witness in the near future.

God's Beasts are shown as far back in as the OT book of Ezekiel in Chapters 1 and 10:

1:10 "And every one had four faces: the first face was the face of a cherub, and the second face was the face of a man, and the third the face of a lion, and the fourth the face of an eagle."

10:14- And every one had four faces: the first face was the face of a cherub, and the second face was the face of a man, and the third the face of a lion, and the fourth the face of an eagle.

Here, the Cherubim also have four faces but one is the face of a cherub instead of an ox (or calf) which symbolizes a servant animal. This was how

Christ was characterized during His 1st Advent. This change in the depiction of the faces could be because what Ezekiel witnessed was the Lord depicted in a different era/dispensational period.

Or, it could be that the prophet in his vision is seeing the "angel of the Lord" (a theophany, or spiritual depiction).

Another possibility is that Ezekiel sees the face of a cherub (angel) rather than an ox because God in his infinite mercy during the Tribulation sends an angel to fly through the atmosphere preaching the Gospel.

The fact that God has Beasts symbolizing the Gospel of Salvation through Jesus, and that John and the 24 Elders are near these Beasts, is another proof of the Pre-Tribulation Rapture. Believers prior to the Tribulation are in Heaven around God's Throne with His Beasts, while others go through the Tribulation at the mercy of the world's Beast and the Satanic powers behind it. As such, instead of being raptured, many of them are martyred.

Martyrs of Revelation 7:9 Clothed in White

Revelation 7:9 is another proof for a pre-Tribulation Rapture and goes with the scarlet color of the Revelation 13 Beast.

"After this I beheld, and, lo, a great multitude, which no man could number, of all nations, and kindreds, and people, and tongues, stood before the throne, and before the Lamb, clothed with white robes, and palms in their hands;"

This chapter verse coincides with the 5th Seal of Revelation 5. This is not a judgment; rather, it shows the Lord's Tribulation martyrs from all nations wearing white robes standing before the Throne and the Lamb.

John a Pre-Trib Believer Doesn't Recognize Martyrs

John needs to be told by one of the 24 Elders who the Tribulation martyrs are, because John is a Pre-Tribulation saint. As a pre-Tribulation believer he and the 24 Elders already have been given white robes while the tribulation believers had to "keep their garments" from being spotted. In Matthew Chapter 22 the Lord gives a parable about a man who is not wearing the proper wedding garment and was cast out of the Lord's presence at the wedding:

Matt. 22:12 "And he saith unto him, Friend, how camest thou in hither not having a wedding garment? And he was speechless."

These martyrs had witnessed of Salvation via the Lord Jesus and were a thorn in the side of the anti-Christ--and the world itself. As such, the sealed Jews were persecuted, betrayed by family members and sent before kings and rulers to testify of Jesus--as He mentioned to them during the Olivet Discourse:

Matt. 24:9-10 "Then shall they deliver you up to be afflicted, and shall kill you: and ye shall be hated of all nations for my name's sake. And then shall many be offended, and shall betray one another, and shall hate one another."

Ultimately, these witnesses were killed, as were those who believed their testimony of Jesus as Savior.

In Revelation 14 v. 3 these Jewish witnesses sing a new song exclusive to themselves. In Chapter 15 v. 2 and 3 the rest of the Tribulation martyrs are in heaven with those who got victory over the Beast. These are both Jew and Gentile as shown by the songs they sing—of Moses (Jewish) and of the Lamb (Jesus):

"And I saw as it were a sea of glass mingled with fire: and them that had gotten the victory over the beast, and over his image, and over his mark, and over the number of his name, stand on the sea of glass, having the harps of God. And they sing the song of <u>Moses</u> the servant of God, and the song of the <u>Lamb</u>, saying, Great and marvellous are thy works, Lord God Almighty; just and true are thy ways, thou King of saints."

It is important to note that these are not the same martyrs shown under the altar in the 5th Seal, but those whom God told these martyrs to wait for, per Revelation 6:11:

"And white robes were given unto every one of them; and it was said unto them, that they should rest yet for a little season, until their fellowservants also and their brethren, that should be killed as they were, should be fulfilled."

The aforementioned is proof of the Pre-Tribulation Rapture, because from this portion of the narrative we can see that there is no rapture mid-Tribulation—or after the Tribulation. These souls are immediately present with the Lord upon death—but they do not have their glorified bodies like those who have been raptured.

God's Wrath Finally Poured Out

Right after this when all the martyred souls are in Heaven, still in Revelation. 15, is when the angels with the 7 last plagues are introduced. The angels are given bowls/vials full of God's wrath. As mentioned before, believers in the Lord Jesus are

"Not appointed to wrath"--neither man's, nor Satan's nor God's.

The events in Revelation 15 occur near the very end of the Tribulation period, as God has shortened the days considerably, per Matthew 24:22:

"And except those days should be shortened, there should no flesh be saved: but for the elect's sake those days shall be shortened."

From this it can be seen that God has waited a l-o-n-g time to pour this out. At this time the Temple in Heaven is filled with God's glory and power so that no man can enter it until the plagues (of wrath) are over. This is opposite of what happened when Jesus died for our sins on the cross: the veil of the Temple in Jerusalem was rent in two, per Matthew 27:51:

"And, behold, the veil of the temple was rent in twain from the top to the bottom; and the earth did quake, and the rocks rent;"

Jesus took all of God's wrath for sin while He was on the cross, so that believers don't need to suffer this fate. Further, His work allowed us to enter into God's presence, per Paul in Hebrews 10:19:

"Having therefore, brethren, boldness to enter into the holiest by the blood of Jesus."

This is another proof of a Pre-Tribulation Rapture.

"It is Done": No Post-Tribulation Rapture

In Revelation 16 v. 17 after the bowls/vials full of God's wrath are emptied a voice from the Temple in Heaven is heard saying "It is done" :

"And the seventh angel poured out his vial into the air; and there came a great voice out of the temple of heaven, from the throne, saying, It is done."

This is the same thing Jesus said on the cross after taking all God's wrath for sin on Himself, per John 19:30:

"When Jesus therefore had received the vinegar, he said, It is finished: and he bowed his head, and gave up the ghost."

Now, at the end of the Tribulation, people who have rejected God's mercy completely are the subject of His wrath. There is no Post-Tribulation Rapture.

As for God's wrath: Not only does God wait patiently to pour this out, but it appears He needs the encouragement from His angels to do so, per Revelation 16: 4-7:

"And the third angel poured out his vial upon the rivers and fountains of waters; and they became blood. And I heard the angel of the waters say, Thou art righteous, O Lord, which art, and wast, and shalt be, because thou hast judged thus. For they have shed the blood of saints and prophets, and thou hast given them blood to drink; for they are worthy. And I heard another out of the altar say, Even so, Lord God Almighty, true and righteous are thy judgments."

One of these angels is probably the same one who encouraged and strengthened Jesus in the Garden of Gethsemane, per Luke 22:42-43:

"Saying, Father, if thou be willing, remove this cup from me: nevertheless not my will, but

thine, be done. And there appeared an angel unto him from heaven, strengthening him."

This is proof that Jesus' followers are not appointed to wrath of the Tribulation.

Mystery Babylon: Confusion

In Revelation 17:5-7 this mystery is described:

"...upon her forehead was a name written, MYSTERY, BABYLON THE GREAT, THE MOTHER OF HARLOTS AND ABOMINATIONS OF THE EARTH. And I saw the woman drunken with the blood of the saints, and with the blood of the martyrs of Jesus: ... And the angel said unto me... I will tell thee the mystery of the woman, and of the beast that carrieth her, which hath the seven heads and ten horns."

Before the Babylonian empire of Nebuchadnezzar there was the Tower of Babel described in Genesis 11:9:

"Therefore is the name of it called Babel; because the LORD did there confound the language of all the earth: and from thence did the

LORD scatter them abroad upon the face of all the earth."

The tower of Babel symbolized man's effort to scale heavenly heights without a moral compass. God had not yet sent His Messiah, so one can imagine the evil that would result from an organized world of un-redeemed peoples speaking the same language. At the Tower of Babel God confused the people's languages. Babylon essentially means confusion. With confusion while being devoid of a foundation based on God's principles we get the world system symbolically called Babylon in Revelation where there are no Christians--followers of Jesus. This is another proof for the Pre-Tribulation Rapture.

Mystery Babylon is initially carried by the Revelation 13 Beast on its crowns, giving it legitimacy. (Mystery Babylon doesn't "ride" the Beast, but is "carried" atop it.) The fact that the word "Harlot" is written on its forehead symbolizes its thought process, just like the 144,000 Jews who have God's seal on their forehead indicates their thought process; just as the Mark of the Beast is given in the forehead (again symbolic of thought process) or on the right hand: the thought process tells the right hand what to do.

Believers Think Opposite of Mystery Babylon

The Holy Spirit in believers changes their thought process, making worldly thoughts captive to Christ. This is in keeping with "names on foreheads" indicating thought process, whether they be God's thoughts or man's or Satan's. In Revelation 22:4 it states of the Lord's followers:

"And they shall see his face; and his name shall be in their foreheads."

The redeemed in Heaven will have the Lord's exact thought process (with variations to suit individual personalities/strengths/interests). As such, they won't be able to sin—much less think a sinful thought. Therefore, they will be able to think fantastic things and then speak these thoughts into existence, just like God did in Genesis 1:4,10,12,18,21,25,31 and declare their creation "good" or "very good."

This is the opposite of Babylon/confusion in Revelation, and of the tower of Babel in Genesis where God needed to stop sinful mankind from having the collective ability to put into existence whatever thoughts came to mind.

Symbolic Harlot: False Religion of Sacrifice

In the same chapter, Revelation 17, this symbolic woman MYSTERY BABYLON is called "MOTHER OF HARLOTS." An unfaithful woman is called a harlot in Scripture. God is not picking on women here. God calls Israel a "her" and he describes her as glorious in Revelation 12:1:

"And there appeared a great wonder in heaven; a woman clothed with the sun, and the moon under her feet, and upon her head a crown of twelve stars:"

In the Old Testament book of Jeremiah 3:6 God said that Israel had become a harlot:

"... in the days of Josiah the king, Hast thou seen that which backsliding Israel hath done? she is gone up upon every high mountain and under every green tree, and there hath played the harlot"

This means that Israel at the time practiced false religions of the nations around her. Time after time Israel was unfaithful, forgetting to abide by God's commandments and looking for help or to make alliances with surrounding countries against her enemies. God claimed that He was their ever present help, yet they didn't believe him.

The Harlot of Revelation is carried upon the Beast. This bears repeating because it shows that the Beast is (at first) approving of the Harlot, which is a false religion. Many believe this to be the Roman Catholic Church (not the people in this church who love Jesus), but this does not fit the context; rather, the Harlot appears to be Israel's revived religion of Sacrifice. Jesus was the once-and-for-all sacrifice for our sins.

Mystery Babylon The Great: Worldly Commercial System

Again in Revelation 17:5 it says of this symbol:

"And upon her forehead was a name written, MYSTERY, BABYLON THE GREAT, THE MOTHER OF HARLOTS AND ABOMINATIONS OF THE EARTH."

Earlier in this Chapter it was said that Babylon the Great of Revelation 18 is the worldly commercial system. This system is so corrupt it sees the selling of "…slaves and the souls of men…"

That Great City: Jerusalem

That great city is said many times in Revelation and this looks to be Jerusalem because Revelation 11:8 says of the two Witnesses God has sent to earth:

"And their dead bodies shall lie in the street of the great city, which spiritually is called Sodom and Egypt, <u>where also our Lord was crucified</u>."

This shows that Israel is the locale of most events that occur during the Tribulation.

Symbolic Sodom and Egypt

The above passage about the two witnesses in Jerusalem also refers to the city as "spiritually called Sodom and Egypt." Sodom was destroyed along with Gomorrah and surrounding cities in Genesis 19. In Ezekiel 16:48 God gives the reason for their destruction while likening Israel's behavior as worse:

"As I live, declares the Lord GOD, Sodom, your sister and her daughters have not done as you and your daughters have done. Behold, this was the guilt of your sister Sodom: she and her daughters had arrogance, abundant food and careless ease, but she did not help the poor and needy. Thus they were haughty and committed abominations before Me. Therefore I removed them when I saw it..."

Egypt is symbolic of bondage (slavery) to sin in general. God delivered His people Israel from bondage with the Passover--a pre-figure of Jesus--the Lamb of God Who took away our sins on the cross. Through this symbolism God is saying that during the 70th week He sees still unrepentant Israel as Sodom and Egypt.

All the above symbols speak of the Tribulation being Jewish in nature and shows most events of the Tribulation occur in Israel. In fact, it appears that the one-world government--the Revelation 13 Beast--is headquartered there, as Ezekiel 28:1-19 speaks of God casting Satan--anti-Christ--out of the mountain of God to earth, and in Revelation we see Satan himself proclaiming himself to be God while he stands in the Temple in Jerusalem.

The Hour that Will Try the Whole World

The "hour" symbolizing the Tribulation/70th Week, while centering on Israel and Jerusalem, will indeed try everyone on earth. Revelation 13:15-17 states:

"And he had power to give life unto the image of the beast, that the image of the beast should both speak, and cause that as many as would not worship the image of the beast should be killed. And he causeth all, both small and great, rich and poor, free and bond, to receive a mark in their right hand, or in their foreheads: And that no man might buy or sell, save he that had the mark, or the name of the beast, or the number of his name."

Earlier Dr. Gerald Stanton stated that God's judgments fall on Gentiles who have rejected Jesus:

"God's judgment falls likewise upon the individual wicked, the kings of the earth, the great, the rich, and the mighty, every bondman and every free man (Rev 6:15-17). It falls upon all who blaspheme the name of God and repent not to give Him glory (Rev. 16:9). Wicked men, godless nations, suffering Israel—these may all be found in Revelation 6-18; but one looks in vain for the church of Christ, which is His body, until he reaches the nineteenth chapter..."

The fact God will make an end of all the nations where the Jews were scattered is another proof of a Pre-Tribulation Rapture. In Jeremiah 46:28 God said:

"Fear thou not, O Jacob my servant, saith the LORD: for I am with thee; for I will make a full end of all the nations whither I have driven thee: but I will not make a full end of thee, but correct thee in measure; yet will I not leave thee wholly unpunished."

This CHAPTER has shown that the 7 Churches are symbolic of the completed church age; John is symbolic of the church; the 24 Elders symbolize all Pre-Tribulation believers—and all these are present in Heaven with the Lord as the Tribulation period plays out on earth.

On earth the Beast of Revelation 13 is the one-world government without God, and the other symbolism shows that the Tribulation narrative centers on the Jewish people in Israel and Jerusalem.

WORKS CITED & SCRIPTURE REFERENCED IN CHAPTER 6

[1] **R.A. Torrey.** What the Bible Teaches, p. 522, Whitaker House; 1 edition (May 7, 2004).

Mark 3:17 And James the son of Zebedee, and John the brother of James; and he surnamed them Boanerges, which is, The sons of thunder:

Rev.17:15 And he saith unto me, The waters which thou sawest, where the whore sitteth, are peoples, and multitudes, and nations, and tongues.

Rev. 13:1-6 And I stood upon the sand of the sea, and saw a beast rise up out of the sea, having seven heads and ten horns, and upon his horns ten crowns, and upon his heads the name of blasphemy. And the beast which I saw was like unto a leopard, and his feet were as the feet of a bear, and his mouth as the mouth of a lion: and the dragon gave him his power, and his seat, and great authority. And I saw one of his heads as it were wounded to death; and his deadly wound was healed: and all the world wondered after the beast. And they worshipped the dragon which gave power unto the beast: and they worshipped the beast, saying, Who is like unto the beast? who is able to make war with him? And there was given unto him a mouth speaking great things and blasphemies; and power was given unto him to continue forty and two months. And he opened his mouth in blasphemy against God, to blaspheme his name, and his tabernacle, and them that dwell in heaven.

Rev. 6:1, 3, 5, 7 And I saw when the Lamb opened one of the seals, and I heard, as it were the noise of thunder, one of the four beasts saying, Come and see. And when he had opened the second seal, I heard the second beast say, Come and see. And when he had opened the third seal, I heard the third beast say, Come and see. And I beheld, and lo a black horse; and he that sat on him had a pair of balances in his hand. And when he had opened the fourth seal, I heard the voice of the fourth beast say, Come and see.

Rev. 4:6   And before the throne there was a sea of glass like unto crystal: and in the midst of the throne, and round about the throne, were four beasts full of eyes before and behind.

Rev. 14:3 And they sung as it were a new song before the throne, and before the four beasts, and the elders: and no man could learn that song but the hundred and forty and four thousand, which were redeemed from the earth.

Gen. 1:4,10,12,18,21,25,31 And God saw the light, that it was good: and God divided the light from the darkness. And God called the dry land Earth; and the gathering together of the waters called he Seas: and God saw that it was good. And the earth brought forth grass, and herb yielding seed after his kind, and the tree yielding fruit, whose seed was in itself, after his kind: and God saw that it was good. And to rule over the day and over the night, and to divide the light from the darkness: and God saw that it was good. And God created great whales, and every living creature that moveth, which the waters brought forth abundantly, after their kind, and every winged fowl after his kind: and God saw that it was good. And God made the beast of the earth after his kind, and cattle after their kind, and every thing that creepeth upon the earth after his kind: and God saw that it was good. And God saw every thing that he had made, and, behold, it was very good. And the evening and the morning were the sixth day.

CHAPTER 7: JESUS THE THIEF RAPTURES HIS FOLLOWERS

- Jesus--The Thief in the Night
- Day of the Lord: Rapture and the Start of the Tribulation
- "Night" Symbolic of Spiritual Darkness
- Night Comes Upon People Unaware
- Believers Walk in the Day

Jesus--The Thief in the Night

Interestingly the way the Lord Jesus is described on the Day of the Lord is as a "thief" (Rev. 3:3; 2 Pet. 3:10). Jesus will forcefully remove (harpazo) His followers away from the spiritually ignorant world, whom Satan is the god of, and this is whom Jesus refers to in the following:

Luke 12:39 ...if the good man of the house had known what hour the thief would come, he would have watched, and not have suffered his house to be broken through."

Day of the Lord: Rapture and the Start of the Tribulation

At the start of the book of Revelation John said he was in the spirit on "the Lord's day."

Therefore to say that the Rapture occurs at the end of the Tribulation does not make sense. Pastor Cornelius R. Stam in "The Day of the Lord, What is it?" which was cited earlier, explains that the Day of the Lord begins with the Tribulation period:

"And...No, the Rapture of the Body of Christ to be with Him will not follow the tribulation; it will precede it. Thus the Apostle Paul, after writing about the Rapture of the Body in I Thessalonians 4, continues in Chapter 5 with the word 'But,' to show the dis relation of God's prophesied 'times and seasons' and 'the day of the Lord,' from that blessed day for which every believer should be 'looking,' 'waiting,' and 'watching.'" [1]

"Night" Symbolic of Spiritual Darkness

The "night" in which Jesus is described as a "thief" is the spiritual darkness of the world that wants nothing to do with Jesus or His Word. Worldly people believe the world needs one leader who can fix everything and bring "peace" or one-world unity. Others believe they are good or religious. These people have a "form of godliness" but deny the power thereof" [2 Tim. 3:5] meaning they speak loftily of "their" great faith in God, but never mention Jesus or the cross, which is what Paul calls *"the power of salvation to those who believe"* [1 Cor. 1:18]. Still, others believe they are "very spiritual" but the Lord said of these people in Matthew 6:23 *"If therefore the light that is in thee be darkness, how great is that darkness!"*

By portraying Himself as a "thief in the night" Jesus is telling us He comes for His followers during a time of (probably great) spiritual darkness.

Night Comes Upon People Unaware

This night is the Tribulation Period--the whole 7 years. Amos 5:20 attests: *"[Shall] not the day of the LORD [be] darkness, and not light? even very dark, and no brightness in it?"*

Believers Walk in the Day

Believers walk in the daytime and the Lord Himself provides the light, per Acts 26:18 :

"To open their eyes, and to turn them from darkness to light, and from the power of Satan unto God, that they may receive forgiveness of sins, and inheritance among them which are sanctified by faith that is in me."

This is in contrast to spiritual darkness which is a result of not "watching" or reading Scripture.

1 Thess. 5:2-7: "For yourselves know perfectly that the day of the Lord so cometh as a thief in the night.... But ye, brethren, are not in darkness, that that day should overtake you as a thief. Ye are all children of light, and the children of the day: we are not of the night, nor of darkness. For they that sleep sleep in the night; and they that be drunken are drunken in the night."

Rev. 3:3 "Remember therefore how thou has received and heard, and hold fast, and repent. If therefore thou shalt not watch, I will come on thee as a thief, and thou shalt not know what hour I will come upon thee."

2 Pet. 3:10 "But the day of the Lord will come as a thief in the night..."

WORKS CITED & SCRIPTURE RFERENCED IN CHAPTER 7

[1] **Pastor Cornelius R. Stam.** "The Day of the Lord, What is it?"https://www.bereanbiblesociety.org/the-day-of-the-lord-what-is-it/

2 Tim. 3:5 Having a form of godliness, but denying the power thereof: from such turn away.

1 Cor. 1:18 For the preaching of the cross is to them that perish foolishness; but unto us which are saved it is the power of God.

CONCLUSION

The word rapture is not in English translations of Scripture, but in the Greek translation the word "harpazo" is used in context of the Lord's "calling up" or "snatching away" His followers from the earth prior to the Tribulation period. Scripture teaches that the Lord's coming/appearing is for His believers only, and this occurs at the Rapture, which is distinct from His 2nd Advent to earth during which time Jesus is accompanied by a great multitude of His followers from Heaven.

Both the Old and New Testaments give many clear proofs of a Pre-Tribulation Rapture, and the book of Revelation itself provides concrete evidence of a Pre-Tribulation Rapture.

Those who insist that the Lord Jesus' followers will have to go through the Tribulation are in spiritual darkness. They lack the Wisdom of God which He gives to those who seek Him and ask for it. Those who seek Him like to read His Word. Those who follow the Lord are not in darkness. We are watching for Him and will be very prepared.

101 (PLUS) PROOFS ENUMERATED

Rapture is for Real
Harpazo translated from the Greek to "raptureo" in Latin
Rapture Not a New Doctrine—Many People Raptured already
Enoch Prophesied of Rapture

3 Signs of Imminent Rapture
Fig Tree—Israel
Jerusalem in Israel's possession
Plans for 3rd Temple
Israel's Enemies want them Destroyed

Paul, Peter & John state Rapture Occurs at Coming/Appearing/Revelation of Jesus to His followers
1 Corinthians 15:51-54
1 Thessalonians 2:19
1 Thess. 5:5
1 Thess. 4:17
1 Timothy 6:14
2 Tim. 1:10
2 Tim. 4:1
2 Tim. 4:8 Raptured given crowns, shown worn in Rev. 4:4 in Heaven
Titus 2:13
1 Peter 1:7

1 Pet. 1:13
1 Pet. 5:21
1 John 3:2

Characteristics of Rapture
Rapture Before and Distinct from Christ's 2nd Advent
Rapture only for Jesus' followers/ "Secret" rapture
The Trumpet Voice: the Rapture Call to "Come up Hither"
Above is "Last Trump" of 1Corinthians
Those who died in Christ before the Rapture Christ Will bring with Him
Believers Saved from Wrath
The Church is the Lord's Bride
Church is the Lord's Body
No Rapture for the General Population who flounder on earth
End of Tribulation: 2nd Advent: Jesus Returns to Earth with all His Raptured Followers
Those on earth try to fight Jesus at His return

Reason for Rapture is opposite of Reason for Tribulation
Church Age Ends, believers Raptured before Trials and Judgment Begin
No Mid-Tribulation Rapture as anti-Christ Persecutes world

No Rapture (or Trumpet Call) after the Tribulation for it is great/terrible Day of the Lord

Rapture Happens on/within "The Day of Christ"
Philippians 1:10
Phil. 2:16
2 Thess. 2:2

Characteristics of the Tribulation
The OT Book of Daniel: Tribulation/70the Week Jewish in nature
The Tribulation is to "Finish the Transgression ..."
7 Years begin with Covenant to Jews
Last 3 ½ years "Time of Jacob's (Israel's) Troubles" not "Church's Troubles"

Old Testament Raptures and Pre-Figures of the Pre-Tribulation Rapture
Enoch Raptured
Noah & Family Delivered
Lot & His 2 Daughters Delivered
Rahab & Family Delivered / Joshua here a "type" of Jesus
Elijah Raptured
Isaiah: Pre-Tribulation Rapture for Saint's Protection
Zechariah prophesies that after Tribulation Raptured Return to Earth with Jesus

New Testament Records Several Individuals Raptured
Jesus Raptured at Ascension
Paul, spokesman for rapture was raptured
John raptured beginning of Revelation
Two Witnesses Raptured at End of Tribulation

Gospels Speak of the Calling up and Away of Christ's followers
The Olivet Discourse (OD)
Matthew 24:37
Matthew 25: The Parable of the 10 Virgins
Luke 21:36
Why John's Gospel Omits the Olivet Discourse (instructions for people not raptured)

Raptures or Saving Out of Judgment Indicates Beginning or Ending of Dispensational Eras
Enoch
Noah
Rahab
Elijah
Jesus
John
Two Witnesses

Specific Statements in Revelation Point to Pre-Tribulation Rapture

"The Lord's Day" in Chapter 1

Jesus Promises to Keep Followers from Tribulation

Jesus says unless lukewarm church type repents, they will go through Tribulation

Different Dispensations/Divisions on Revelation

4 Divs.: each diff. "dispensation"

Chapter 1: Change of Speakers/Locale

Chapter 2: Change of Speaker/Locale

Chapter 3: Change of Speakers and Change of Locale

Parenthetical Structure of 6-18: Church Not Mentioned Throughout

Chapter 12: About Israel, not the Church

144,000 Witnesses of Revelation 7 are Jewish—Church is gone (raptured)

144,000 are Martyred for their Testimony of Jesus

Two Witnesses in Jerusalem only witnesses left on earth

Angels flying through Atmosphere with Gospel

Chapter 19: "After these things…" the Tribulation, which John (all believers) witness from Heaven

Chapter 19: The Church is Christ's Heavenly Bride Who Returns to Earth with Him

Symbolism in Revelation
John Symbolic of All Believers
The 7 Spirits are Complete Work of Holy Spirit in the Church
7 Churches Symbolize Complete Church Age
24 Elders Symbolize All the Redeemed
Old Testament Pre-Figure of 24 Elders
Symbolic Harlot: False Religion of Sacrifice upheld by worldly system
Mystery, Babylon the Great: corrupt worldly commercial system
That Great City: Jerusalem—Tribulation Jewish in nature
Symbolic Sodom and Egypt—Tribulation Jewish in nature
God's Wrath Finally Poured Out--Believers not appointed to this wrath

Conditions on Earth after Rapture/During Tribulation
The Hour that Will Try the Whole World—Tribulation affects whole un-redeemed world
The Beast of Revelation Chapter 13 is Entire Un-Redeemed World
Satan is Behind the Beast
The Beast is Scarlet--Symbolic of Sin
Anti-Christ is "Little Horn" per Daniel—persecutes Jews

Mystery Babylon: Confusion: Believers think Opposite of Babylon

"It is Done": No Post-Tribulation Rapture

Conditions in Heaven during Tribulation

God's Beasts are Counter to the World's Beast, symbolize redemption via Jesus

Tribulation Martyrs of Revelation 7:9 Clothed in White

Different song (of Moses) sung by redeemed Jews

John a Pre-Tribulation Believer Doesn't Recognize Tribulation Martyrs

Conditions on Earth right before and at Rapture

Restrainer (Holy Spirit on earth and in believers) holding back Beast & Lawlessness

Jesus--The Thief in the Night raptures His followers

"Night" Symbolic of Spiritual Darkness

Night Comes Upon People Unaware but Believers Walk in the Day

SOURCES & REFERENCES

King James Version (KJV) of the Bible. All Scripture referenced and cited is from the King James Version

Strong's Concordance harpazó: to seize, catch up, snatch... obtain by robbery...snatch up, suddenly and decisively – like someone seizing bounty (spoil, a prize); to take by an open display of force (i.e. not covertly or secretly). http://biblehub.com/greek/726.htm

HARPAZO the KJV New Testament Greek Lexicon. Greek lexicon based on Thayer's and Smith's Bible Dictionary plus others; this is keyed to the large Kittel and the "Theological Dictionary of the New Testament." http://www.biblestudytools.com/lexicons/greek/kjv/harpazo.html

Merriam-Webster Dictionary. http://www.merriam-webster.com/dictionary/rapture

Pastor Cornelius R. Stam. The Day of the Lord — What Is It? On September 2, 2001 @ 8:57 pm https://www.bereanbiblesociety.org/the-day-of-the-lord-what-is-it/

Sir Robert Anderson. The Coming Prince: The Marvelous Prophecy of Daniel's Seventy Weeks Concerning the Antichrist, Published by Cosimo Classics (December 1, 2007)

Dr. Gerald Stanton. Archived on Rapture Ready
http://www.raptureready.com/resource/stanton/gerald_stanton.html/

Wikipedia. Yeshua (ישוע, with vowel pointing יֵשׁוּעַ – yēšūăʿ in Hebrew) was a common alternative form of the name יְהוֹשׁוּעַ "(Yehoshuah" – Joshua) in later books of the Hebrew Bible and among Jews of the Second Temple period. Meaning "salvation" in Hebrew, it was also the most common

form of the name Jesus hence the name corresponds to the Greek spelling Iesous, from which, through the Latin Iesus, comes
the English spelling Jesus. Main article: Names and titles of Jesus in the New Testament Yeshua in Hebrew is a verbal derivative from "to rescue", "to deliver"
https://en.wikipedia.org/wiki/Yeshua_%28name%29

Ray C. Stedman. The Silent Years: THE 400 YEARS BETWEEN THE OLD AND NEW TESTAMENTS
http://ldolphin.org/daniel/silentyears.html

Pastor Chuck Smith. The Rapture of the Church, Through The Bible C2000 Series on The Word For Today
http://www.thewordfortoday.org

Wesley's and People's Notes on Rev. 16:15.
The Bible, KJV
http://www.kingjamesbibleonline.org/

R.A. Torrey. What the Bible Teaches, p. 522, Whitaker House; 1 edition (May 7, 2004).

READER'S NOTES

READER'S NOTES

Printed in Great Britain
by Amazon